Your Wide Awakening

A Guide to Anorexia Recovery

Jensy Scarola

BALBOA.
PRESS
A DIVISION OF HAY HOUSE

Copyright © 2013 Jensy Scarola.

All rights reserved. No part of this book may be used or reproduced by any means, graphic, electronic, or mechanical, including photocopying, recording, taping or by any information storage retrieval system without the written permission of the publisher except in the case of brief quotations embodied in critical articles and reviews.

Balboa Press books may be ordered through booksellers or by contacting:

Balboa Press
A Division of Hay House
1663 Liberty Drive
Bloomington, IN 47403
www.balboapress.com
1-(877) 407-4847

Because of the dynamic nature of the Internet, any web addresses or links contained in this book may have changed since publication and may no longer be valid. The views expressed in this work are solely those of the author and do not necessarily reflect the views of the publisher, and the publisher hereby disclaims any responsibility for them.

The author of this book does not dispense medical advice or prescribe the use of any technique as a form of treatment for physical, emotional, or medical problems without the advice of a physician, either directly or indirectly. The intent of the author is only to offer information of a general nature to help you in your quest for emotional and spiritual well-being. In the event you use any of the information in this book for yourself, which is your constitutional right, the author and the publisher assume no responsibility for your actions.

Any people depicted in stock imagery provided by Thinkstock are models, and such images are being used for illustrative purposes only.
Certain stock imagery © Thinkstock.

Printed in the United States of America.

ISBN: 978-1-4525-7935-1 (sc)
ISBN: 978-1-4525-7937-5 (hc)
ISBN: 978-1-4525-7936-8 (e)

Library of Congress Control Number: 2013914053

Balboa Press rev. date: 08/13/2013

For my angels, Lindsay and Jillian, the sunshine and sugar of my life.
I am very lucky to be your mommy. I will always love you.

Contents

Acknowledgments ix
Introduction xi

I. Mind
Chapter 1: Why Do We Have Eating Disorders? 1
Chapter 2: Nature vs. Nurture 11
Chapter 3: Self-Love 17

II. Body
Chapter 4: Wide-Awake Eating 35
Chapter 5: Wide-Awake Body Movement 47

III. Spirit
Chapter 6: Relationships 55
Chapter 7: Exploring Your Spirituality 67

IV. Connecting Mind, Body, and Spirit
Chapter 8: Healing Your Life through Chakra Balancing 79
Chapter 9: Fulfilling Your Passion, Living Your Purpose, and Experiencing Joy! 113

Epilogue 119

List of Illustrations

mountain
bridge
standing forward bend
bound angle pose
low squat pose
wide angle seated forward bend
bow
standing split pose
boat
camel
cobra
cow
bridge
supported shoulder stand
fish pose
child's pose
dolphin
yoga mudra
corpse
half lotus
legs up the wall

Acknowledgments

First and foremost, I would like to thank my dad for always believing in me, standing by me, and loving me unconditionally. You have never let me down. I will treasure our deep and meaningful talks—especially at Grotto Pizza in Newark, Delaware, every Monday, at the height of my disease. You have supported every decision I have ever made. You are my greatest role model—father, mother, friend, and teacher all rolled into one very special man. I love you.

To my soul mate, Lenny: we forged our lifelong bond at age sixteen. Your love for me has never wavered. You have supported me through thick and thin, watched me suffer, and watched me fly. You have always believed in my dreams and carried me on your shoulders. I am eternally grateful for our love.

To my big sisters, Melanie and Missy: thank you for your endless pep talks full of encouragement and support. Thank you for giving me a soft place to fall when I needed it the most. You have inspired me to be a better woman—a better mom, spouse, daughter, friend, and sister.

To Lindsay and Jillian: you are my greatest teachers and sources of inspiration. You have taught me more than you can ever imagine. You are the light in my world. Your daily musings and belly laughs lift my spirit every day. I'm a very lucky mommy to have daughters like you. I will continue to fight for you and love you forever and ever.

To my extended family—Linda, Elly, Jay, Sonne, Nancy, and Nona: you have been a huge support; been there for our family when we needed it the most; and loved me through it all. I am indebted to you for your endless support. I love you.

To my stepbrothers and sisters—Drew and Mary Madison, Tucker and Kristin, and Nicki: thank you for loving me despite my flaws, and for allowing me to be a part of your lives.

To Kevin and Jeff, my surrogate big brothers. You have deeply cared for me for all these years; listened to my moans and groans; and have been like brothers to me, always making me smile.

To my nieces and nephews—Emma, Katie, Sara, Grace, Jack, Brendan, Sean, Shane, Lily, Callie, and Clay: you are like sons and daughters to me. You give me the gift of your joy, and I get to bask in the glow of your light. I will love you always.

To my dearest childhood friends—Kristin, Katie, and Erin: for standing by me throughout all these years and supporting me every step of the way, even during my darkest days. You inspire me to be a better friend. I am grateful for the bond of sisterhood we have shared.

To my soul sisters—Jen, Tanya, Kate: thank you for your inspiration, your love, our long talks, and your support. Our friendships will last forever.

To Father Kevin Nadolski for always being there with me in spirit. You have always believed in me, my husband, and my family. You were my first helpful hero and the first person outside my family who believed in my Light.

And to other extended family members and friends, too many to mention: thank you for believing in me and inspiring me to be a better woman. Your grace continues to guide me.

And finally to my mother. You gave me the wings to fly. I know you had something to do with the fact that all these people in my life have encouraged me to never stop flapping my wings. Although we had a short time together, your kind soul and sensitive heart were what inspired me to write this book. I love you so much, and I hope I make you proud. Until we meet again . . .

Introduction

In reading this book, you will learn how to heal an eating disorder; you will discover the tools you will need to overcome any type of adversity, relapse, or setback; and you will come to understand how to apply the tricks, detailed plans, and principles I have applied in my own recovery. I have streamlined my journey so that you can follow along simply and effortlessly. This book will help you find your way, practice self-love, develop your intuition, and maintain healthy, long-lasting relationships. You can heal yourself!

If you are suffering with body image issues, eating disorders, or are engaging in yo-yo dieting, this book will help you. Even if you simply feel unfulfilled, this book can help you. You don't have to be clinically diagnosed with an eating disorder. Deep emotional pain can exist, no matter what the medical world says. Food issues, poor body image, and negative self-talk can wreak havoc in your life.

This book's purpose is not to *change* you but to inspire you. You are good enough as you are. Your eating disorder is not who you are. It's just a disease you have. It is not you. You are not anorexia. You *have* anorexia.

This book will remind you that you are magnificent and that you have something special to offer to the world. That is something we are all born with. I hope the book awakens you in ways that inspire you to begin to love yourself wholly, unconditionally, and bravely, without the influence of dogma, religion, politics, fashion, family demands and expectations, size, or skin color. It's a return to self-love, the greatest love of all.

The book is divided into four parts. In chapters 1-3, we explore the mind. We will discuss why we have eating disorders, why some people are more susceptible to them, and how to heal through self-love. In chapters 4 and 5, we work on appreciating and loving the body through healthy nourishment and physical activity. We make a connection to our spirit through our relationships, a connection to a higher source, and, in chapters 6 and 7, through an introduction to meditation. Finally, in chapters 8 and 9, we integrate everything we have learned throughout the book to connect the mind, body, and spirit. We investigate chakra healing, which uses yoga poses, meditation, and healing practices to quiet the mind and release old emotional pain stored in the cells of the body. Chapter 9 shows us how to find our true calling and pursue it.

At the end of each chapter, there is a space for you to reflect on what you have read, what you can take from it, and what changes you can make in your life to feel happier.

My wish for you, when you finish this book, is for you to realize that you matter. Your pulse alone tells us that you are here for a reason. You are truly a miracle and have so much to offer the world. I hope this awakens you to recognize your radiant beauty, inside and out. You don't have to battle an eating disorder any longer. We are all on our own journeys, growing and learning and becoming all we were intended to be. Stay strong and may God continue to bless you!

March 16, 1992

I loved the family room in the home I grew up in. I helped my mom redecorate it. The room had plush, blue-and-white striped couches, many cozy pillows filled with goose down, a new cream-colored Berber carpet, many books and pictures, and a ton of family memories. But what I was about to find out that spring day, would turn the family room into my young mother's bedroom in a few short weeks. She sat on the edge of the fireplace that afternoon telling my older twin sisters and me that she had been diagnosed with breast cancer at the very young age of forty-two.

From that day on, the family room became a haven for visitors, a bedroom filled with pill bottles, religious books, cards, a place to eat dinner, and a place to have my last deep and meaningful conversations with my mother. It had been transformed from a safe place where I could unwind and watch television with my family into a hospital room.

Life marched on as usual for me as a fifteen-year-old sophomore in high school while my mom battled breast cancer. I kept busy with friends, sports, school work, and a new boyfriend. My older twin sisters were in their final year of high school and were getting ready to attend college in the fall. My dad continued to work, although much of his time was driving my mom to chemotherapy and radiation appointments downtown.

June 24, 1992

My dad and I went to take my driver's license test on my sixteenth birthday. I was excited to be taking on this new experience. I ended up failing the parallel parking portion of the test—Good grief! Who parallel parks perfectly on the first try? Well, certainly not me!—which meant no license. I would have to try again a few days later. I cried all the way home. When I walked in my home that day, I will never forget the sorrow I saw on my mom's face. She was so sad for me. The last thing I wanted was to let her down.

In the few short months since her diagnosis, my mom had lost all her hair after undergoing her first several rounds of chemotherapy. The cancer had spread to her bones in the lower portion of her spine. The doctors were pursuing more drastic measures and some clinical trials. The radiation was burning my mom from the inside out, including her spirit.

I kept living like a normal, rebellious (somewhat hormonal), grumpy teenage girl while my mom was dying. Quite frankly, I was in denial.

End of August 1992

It was near the end of the summer, and we were moving my sisters into their dormitory at college. They were best friends and have a deep and loving bond to this day, so they had decided to attend the same school and live together. We pulled up to their dormitory with double the belongings. Their room was on the third floor, so that meant walking up and down several flights of stairs many, many times. My mom could barely walk and was doubled over in pain most of the time. She spent the day trying to get comfortable, shifting from a sitting position to lying down to being hunched over on the lower bunk of my sisters' bed. I remember feeling so many emotions, but mostly I was angry—angry at my mom, angry at my sisters for leaving me alone, and just plain angry about the unfairness of life. After unpacking all my sisters' stuff, we pulled away from their new home that day. My sisters had each other. But I knew that, from that point on, my life would never be the same.

My junior year of high school was starting the following week. I was excited to be playing volleyball that fall, but I ended up not being very good at it. In hindsight, I never worked at it the way I work at things now, and frankly, it was an escape from thinking about or being around the misery that surrounded me. I had fun playing with my friends, and Lord knows I needed some fun in my life!

Each day, when I came home from school, there would be a visitor, a home-cooked meal from a neighbor, several get-well cards waiting for my mom in the mailbox, and a new plan for health. It could be a new spiritual path, a new and better chemotherapy regimen, or a new medicine. I chose to avoid it all and focus all my attention on my friends, my boyfriend, and escaping into mindless TV, shopping, and drama. I still was not seeing that, as each day passed, my mom was growing weaker and weaker. The doctors told us that the cancer had now spread to her skull.

October 3, 1992

My sisters were coming home for a visit! My mom was feeling really bad that day. We were now battling cancer that had spread to her liver. We were going to have a spiritual medium come to our home and speak in tongues over my mom in hopes that the cancer would leave her body peacefully in a spontaneous remission. We were trying anything and everything! After the mass was performed in our family room, I had to take my sisters back to school. I was going to spend the night there at their school and experience college life. One of my sisters drove my car and got a speeding ticket on the way there. Looking back, my sisters and I needed an escape! We were kids, for goodness' sake!

Week of October 4, 1992

They admitted my mom into the hospital that Wednesday. I remember staying home alone at night while my dad stayed at the hospital. Sometimes I would sleep at friends' houses so I could get to school more quickly in the mornings. Other times, I would sleep in the basement of our house. I would stay on the phone all night talking with friends to distract myself from everything going on around me.

On Sunday, October 11, one of my girlfriends and I went to the hospital to visit my mom. We got lost getting to the hospital. We were driving down one-way streets the wrong way, blasting our music to the highest of decibels and giggling at our adventure. We finally made it but only stayed for a bit. My mom was weak, cold, and frail. Mostly, she was not even conscious. She told me she loved me very much, asked a few questions about school, and then closed her eyes. I knew she was tired, so we left. My dad continued to stay with her. My friend and I headed back home. We slept in the family room that night and the night after. I was tired, very tired.

October 13, 1992

My dad called the house before 7:00 a.m. and instructed me to drop my friend off at school. I drove into the city that day to spend the day with my mom at the hospital. *Sure*, I thought, *no school!*

When I walked into her hospital room, my mom wasn't talking, moving, or smiling. I gave her a bunch of kisses and stayed with her all morning. My dad asked me to hold her hand to keep her blood pressure down, as it had been running high most of the morning. He needed to do some errands, so I was left in the room with her by myself. I remember thinking, *She's going to be fine; let's get her white blood cell count up (she was battling an infection) and get her up and walking again.* We would be back home in no time. Life would be back to normal.

As morning faded into afternoon, more nervous activity began occurring in the room. Nurses came in and out of the room smiling at me and introducing themselves to me. They already knew so much about me and my family! My mom was always so proud of us. My dad came back in and told me I had done a good job—that by holding Mom's hand I was keeping her calm and happy. He also said that my sisters were leaving school to come to the hospital to be with us. I was glad to see them.

When they got there, they held her hands and hugged and kissed her. I hadn't eaten lunch yet, so I asked one of my sisters to come eat pizza with me. We sat quietly together as I quickly ate my lunch. Then we went back up to my mom's room, where there were more visitors. All of my mom's dear friends, as well as her parents and doctors, were with her now.

My mom was in and out of consciousness most of the afternoon. My dad pulled my sisters and me aside and told us the news I never wanted to hear: this would be my mom's final day. She was dying. Today. I remember watching my sister Missy go to the window sill to sit and cry. I still couldn't believe what I was hearing. My dad asked us to say our good-byes and be at her bedside as she made her transition.

As she passed, my mom was in and out of consciousness, mumbling softly, "I love you, I love you, I love you." I treasure her final words and will hold them in my heart forever. We said the same precious words over and over to her so she knew it was okay to leave us. I will never, ever, forget that my moment in my life. My mom's doctor was at the end of the bed. We would turn to him every minute or so and ask, "Was that it? Was that her last breath?" She would take a breath every thirty seconds, or so it seemed. They were loud and strong, and with each one I still had hope. I still had hope that this was all a dream. It wasn't. And then that was it. She didn't take another one.

She was gone.

My mom left us around 5:30 p.m. on a cool, crisp October day. My dad, my sisters, and I were sobbing and screaming cries of anger, disbelief, and sorrow. I felt stabbing pains in my head, stomach, and jaw. I watched my mom lie motionless on the bed, knowing I would never again feel her warmth or her touch or hear her voice again. Our world had just come crashing down.

I honestly did not know what to do with myself. I didn't know whether I should sit, stand, scream, cry, or run away. I wish I could describe a certain emotion that I was feeling at the time, but I would imagine that shock allows time to stand still, and your brain just shuts down.

My sister offered to drive my car home an hour after my mom's passing. The hospital staff told us to say our final good-byes. I remember going through the motions but not really meaning it. It was a very surreal experience, where I felt as though I were in someone else's body. It was as though I thought she would wake up, and it was all just a very bad dream.

On our way home, I sobbed. My sister sobbed too, but she always had a way of soothing me in times of need. She reassured me that everything would be fine, while we listened to songs we both loved. When we arrived home, friends and family had already gathered. My friends were calling to come over. My sisters' college friends were already there. I didn't really feel like staying in the house, so my friends and I took a walk outside in my neighborhood, which included a golf course.

A guy in my class at school, on whom I had a bit of a crush, came over that night too. His name was Lenny. Lenny and I laid on the golf course looking up at the stars, chatting and laughing. He had a real knack for making me laugh. The laughter was something I needed desperately at the time. He was the perfect distraction.

I really have no recollection of that week, after everyone left. One of the few things I remember is picking out my mom's burial outfit for the viewing. This outfit would be her final outfit as she was laid to rest.

My family always came to me for fashion advice. I remember feeling very honored that I was to pick out the outfit. I chose a coordinated purple shirt, cardigan, and skirt that she had bought from Talbots. My mom had treated herself (which she rarely did) to a stunning, high-priced ensemble. I will never forget the day she brought it home to show me. It matched perfectly. Her eyes sparkled when she pulled it out of the bag.

The Viewing

I chose a black dress of my mother's to wear that evening. It was entirely too big, but I didn't care. It was something to wear, and I wore it to honor her. It was just perfect. I stood by her casket the entire time, greeting loved ones with a hello and a hug. What could I say? Nothing. I had no words that night. I felt sorry for my family and for myself. I was a mess. I was putting on a brave face when all I wanted to do was lie in my bed and cry. At that moment, life seemed to be so unfair. I was feeling pain at the thought of not growing up with my mom and not having her help me pick my husband, my wedding dress, spoil my kids, and meet over lunch with a side of salsa and chips. (Our fave!) I had a big knot in my throat, and I was filled with a myriad of emotions. The next day, I would have to face the funeral and lay my young mom to rest. To me, it felt unreal. Was this really happening?

Pulling into the church parking lot, I saw one of my elementary school classmates. I was so honored that she had chosen to come. I hadn't seen her in years. Many old friends, new friends, teachers, and kids made their way to the church that day. It felt good to be supported and loved by so many and by the fact that people took time out of their lives to honor her life.

Walking into the church, I didn't leave my dad's side. Ugh. What a morning! The church was packed. People came from all over to honor my mother. My sisters read the eulogy, and what a eulogy it was! Beautiful, eloquent, and a perfect testament to what an inherently good person/mom/wife/daughter/friend she was. My dad and I sobbed uncontrollably as we listened to them speak. I really started to feel the impact that my mom's death would have on our family.

Following the Mass, we had to drive about an hour to her burial site. My sisters and I looked on at the procession. We were amazed by how long it was! The love and pride we felt for our mom distracted us during the long ride.

And that was it. She was laid to rest that Friday.

I buried my mom a few months after my sixteenth birthday. My sensitive little heart was shattered into a million tiny pieces.

The next few years are a blur. The blur was the result of my stuffing down my feelings and not facing my emotions about my mother's death. I could never truly be present because I was hurting. Most people think that, a year or two after a traumatic experience like this one, you are supposed to be over it or getting on with your life. It is certainly possible, but that wasn't the case for me. The only way you can move on is if you express your emotions and allow yourself to heal. Allow yourself time to grieve, mourn the loss, and be sad. I didn't know that, and I certainly did not do any of that. I carried on with my high school activities of classes, sports, boys, and going out to numb out. Everyone in my family seemed to be picking up the pieces. My dad starting dating the following year. My sisters were doing great in college; they had wonderful friends and were getting a strong education. I, on the other hand, was feeling lost and lonely.

I entered college in the fall of 1994. My freshman year was a rip-roaring good time. I was happy and really enjoying the freedom of being away from home and learning new things! I had an awesome dormitory and lived with the greatest group of people. We went to fraternity parties, stayed out way too late most nights, ate Ramen noodles, and experienced life on our own for the first time. I continued to date my future husband on and off throughout the year. We continued a long-distance relationship. It was rocky, to say the least, but we were in love and were forging our lifelong bond.

My second semester in college, I joined a sorority with extraordinarily beautiful and smart women. I enjoyed my first few months in the sorority, going to parties, formals, and meeting all kinds of new people. Then school let out for the summer. I went home and got a great job as a hostess at a local restaurant. In the fall of my sophomore year, I moved into the sorority house with about fifty women. We ate dinner together every night in the basement. As the semester went on, I noticed some peculiar dining habits. Some of the girls were dipping vegetables in ketchup and eating dry salads with no dressing and nothing else on their plates. Little by little, they began to waste away. Anorexia, bulimia, overexercising, and unhealthy eating behaviors were running rampant in our house. Instead of trying to help these women, I wanted to be more like them. In an odd way, I admired them.

I was usually the first one down in the kitchen for dinner at 4:00 p.m. Our dining manager made soup and salad first and offered it early, before dinner. I remember grabbing the soup and bread, going up to my room, watching an episode of MTV's *Singled Out* (oh, I know—dreadful and mindless—but funny—television, to say the least!), and waiting for my roommate to get home from class so we could eat together. I never worried about what food I was eating, how my body looked, or what size I wore. I was defined by my love, laughter, spunk, wit, silliness, sensitivity, and friendship. During the second semester of my sophomore year, things began to change. I was feeling left out, common, and ugly, and my self-esteem—which was fragile to begin with—began to whittle away. Being surrounded by gorgeous, smart, funny women all the time made me feel not "enough," so I began to engage in unhealthy eating habits to be enough. I felt everything was wrong with me, from my looks to my clothes to the courses I was taking in college. I just wanted to fade away. I needed my mom to talk me out of the negative thoughts I was feeling about myself. I needed, finally, to grieve her loss and take full responsibility for my actions. I needed to mature into a young woman and face the truth about my life. I was almost twenty years old. It was time for me to grow up. Well, I didn't. I chose an eating disorder instead of life. I chose to hide. I chose to be a coward instead of being courageous. I chose not to seek help; instead, I chose isolation.

I began controlling my calories and started to exercise more frequently. I had a grand plan to take an exercise class for college credits so I would *have* to work out. Many of my sorority sisters were runners and gym rats. I was inspired by the attention they were getting from guys; they looked great and seemed to be truly happy. The exercise class met twice a week. Well, I began to realize that that was simply not enough to shed the kind of weight I wanted to lose.

I want to remind you that I never had weight to lose in the first place.

I wasn't stick skinny. I was well proportioned, toned, and healthy, but I felt that I needed to be thinner to have people like me, accept me, and/or admire me. I felt as though no one loved me. I had lost a huge unconditional source of love and encouragement when I lost my mom. In a way, I felt like an orphan. So I began to go to the gym for ninety minutes a day. I would jump from bike to treadmill to StairMaster and back again. The soup at mealtime was replaced by just bread. I stocked fat-free items (How gross were those? Chips with Olestra? *Gah!*) in my room, and I bought laxatives. I never really lost any weight, but I started to look skinny, probably because I had no vitamins or nutrients in my body. My clothes became looser because I was dehydrated. I started to party five nights out of seven, drinking alcohol every evening and still managing to get to class and pass tests. I didn't know it, but this was the beginning of my checking out of my life . . . I was developing an eating disorder.

That summer, I continued to eat bread for meals, take laxatives, and discovered diet soda to occupy my stomach, hands, and mouth. I joined a gym near my house and would put hot sauce on everything. (Don't you know it speeds up your metabolism? Oh, for the love of God—some of the stupid things I believed!) I began to withdraw from social outings. Eating regularly and looking in the mirror became extremely difficult. I began to look at myself as an ugly monster. I began to hate me. Everything about me.

My junior year started off very well, yet I was still suffering. I changed my major and enjoyed it. I got a terrific job working for my college. Things were becoming great, academically, or so it seemed.

The personal side, however, was continuing to take a turn for the worse. I joined a gym about twenty-five minutes from the sorority house. Working part time and spending hours at the gym gave me the excuse to isolate even more. Between classes, studying, gym, and work, there wasn't much time to eat or socialize. I began to survive on diet soda, raisins, lollipops, and broccoli. On the way to the gym, I would stop at the Chinese restaurant and have them make me a plate of steamed broccoli (no butter and no sauce) and then head to the gym. After spending twenty minutes on the StairMaster, I would spend fifty minutes on the treadmill and then thirty minutes on the recumbent bike. I would finish with abdominal exercises and light weights. (Superlight, because, you know, lifting weights makes you big and husky like a man, right? Riiiiiiight.) When I finished there, I would drive to the 7-Eleven across the street, buy a Super Big Gulp filled with diet soda and two packs of sugar-free gum. That was my dinner. Then I would drive home to sleep in my bed, hungry, very hungry . . . and so alone. I was anorexic.

I managed to waste away to eighty-nine pounds from a healthy one hundred fifteen that year. I lost the hair on my head, grew thick hair on my arms, wore clothes way too big for me, and was cold all the time. I was an anorexic, and yes, now I was different. I had the control so many struggle for with food. I felt defiantly powerful, and *that* gave me purpose. (It's so wickedly twisted; it amazes me to this day that my head worked like that!)

There were many, many days when I wanted to die. My days felt endless, with no relief in sight. I would sob in front of the mirror, calling myself ugly, stupid, an awful person, and a fat, worthless piece of crap. I would stare at every imperfection on my body . . . squeezing the skin, picking at my face, pulling my hair out, weighing myself at least twenty-five times a day, and making this disease my sole purpose for getting up in the mornings. I was determined to weigh less than the day before. I was committing emotional and physical suicide.

Looking back, I should have taken a sabbatical from college and entered an inpatient facility to treat anorexia. I was a mess! I had lost all my friends, my grades were average, and I was morbidly depressed. I gained back the physical weight my senior year, but I was still carrying so much emotional weight. I still needed to heal.

I graduated from college with good grades and normal weight, and everyone thought I was on the path to recovery. "Thought" being the key word here. I am sure the ones closest to me knew I was still engaging in self-destructive habits. I moved back in with my dad after college, got a job in the city, and enjoyed the single nightlife. I still wasn't eating "right," but to me and everyone else, my weight was okay.

The following year, I got engaged to the guy who made me laugh that night on the golf course. Yes, my high school soul mate, Lenny! We made it! We got married a year later. He was and is the only man who has ever loved me unconditionally, despite flaws, eating disorders, emotional baggage, etc. He loved me all through the anorexia days and made my days brighter with his wit, charm, and generosity.

A year later, I went back to school to study Health Promotion. I wrote papers on eating disorders, behavior change, how to prevent eating disorders, and how to recover from them. I worked with teachers on developing programs for the prevention of eating disorders. Unfortunately, there was still a part of me that didn't want to let anorexia go. It seemed like the only thing I knew how to do well. So I didn't finish my degree. I didn't feel authentic, as I was still struggling with the disease. Anorexia prevented me from finishing anything. It's an extremely time-consuming disease that takes over 90 percent of your daily thoughts.

Next, Lenny and I bought our first home and started a family nine months later. I worked out throughout my entire pregnancy. I wrote love letters to the unborn child, I wept a lot, ate healthily, and quit my job halfway through the pregnancy. I was eating healthfully for my unborn child, but I still harbored the fear of gaining too much weight, being ugly, and not "adequate." I had a scary birth with my little angel, but we managed an emergency C-section with a happy ending: a happy and healthy baby girl!

The first night at home with my Lindsay Marie was interesting. I had no idea what to do! (Do any of us?)

We came home from the hospital and were greeted by my dad and his wife and many cards, a lot of flowers and food, and a great many smiles! I remember feeling healthy but scared. What was I gonna do? Could I go to the bathroom by myself? Would I ever sleep again? Would I be sitting at home all day? Was this little girl gonna love me? Did anybody love me? Was I worthy to be the mother of this beautiful miracle? When it was bedtime, I panicked. Where would she sleep? I didn't want to be away from her for one second. I told my dad, his wife, and my husband that I was fine; they should go to bed upstairs, and I would sleep downstairs with Lindsay. When they went to bed, the tears poured. I mean *poooured*. I was a mom. Where was mine?

My mom had been gone for thirteen years by this time. Being parented seemed worlds away, but I needed her, *right now*. I sobbed for hours. My heart literally ached. I fed Lindsay when she cried and rocked her to sleep when she needed to be. I did my best rendition of the Carpenters' "Close to You" when she wouldn't settle. That night, I didn't sleep. I rested her on my chest and listened to her humming, soothing breaths while I thought to myself, repeatedly, *Mom, where are you? Where are you? I need you!*

The first six months were fun. I loved dressing Lindsay up in little outfits, taking her to baby gym classes, and watching her grow. I learned slowly and surely how to satisfy her needs. We spent much time at home napping, feeding, changing diapers, and playing. I was still in a state of depression, but she gave me hope, unconditional love, and a smile I couldn't wait to see every day. When she was six months, I started to lose my appetite, lose weight, and feel even more fatigued and depressed. After about two months, I had lost ten pounds for unknown reasons. I looked and felt terrible. I thought I was dying of something! I never went to the doctor, but my intuition told me to go buy a pregnancy test. Well, I bought seven, and yes, all were positive. I was eleven weeks pregnant.

That pregnancy was a delightful surprise. God had a plan for our little family! I was excited to have babies close together in age, like my sisters and me. I wrote to the baby in my journal while Lindsay napped. I was grateful to have become pregnant, but the truth is, I was feeling really lonely and depressed at home. I missed my mom and still wasn't sure whether I was a good mom. Now I was having another little girl!

Jillian Elle was born in early January. She was an angel baby. She slept well, fed well, and was a happy, smiley ball of love. She was content most of the time and loved her bouncy chair. Lindsay was exploring and learning new things every day. Lenny and I were busy parents. He worked late nights. I, on the other hand was still feeling terribly lonely. I missed my mom. I yearned for her support, her help, and, quite frankly, I wanted a mom to hold me and tell me that everything would be great and that I was doing a great job.

I was in need of love and nurturing myself, so it was hard to give it. We hired a nanny, so I could go back to work. I thought I could pull myself out of depression if I had a career. I started to work with one of my friends, promoting health and wellness at our local schools. It felt good to give back. Still, I didn't feel fulfilled. Although I was very passionate about the work I was doing, it still did not seem right or the job I was really searching for. A few months later I started to spiral downward, hormonally, emotionally, and physically. I started not to care about my appearance, my relationships, and my sense of self worth. *Again!* My life felt like it had no meaning. I felt like a terrible mom, sister, spouse, and friend. Here I was, going back down the anorexia hole again. I would spend hours telling myself that I didn't deserve this life and that I simply did not want live. I felt hopeless about beating anorexia, helpless in being a good mother, and plain worn out. I was sick and tired of fighting my inner demons and feeling worthless. I thought several times a day about taking my own life. A teeny, tiny, little voice inside me told me I still wanted to live. To this day, I marvel that I listened to it. This is why I believe in a Higher Power, and this is how my faith was reborn. My girls were everything to me. Their bright, cheerful faces are what kept me going and what keep me going to this very day.

So I picked up the phone one day and called a treatment center for eating disorders. No one made the call for me. I did it. I was ready to get serious about healing!

I was gonna beat this disease once and for all. If not for me, for my amazing husband, family, friends, and, most of all, for my gorgeous baby girls! To be a mother is a privilege, not a right. I was going to fight for them. Their love and light carried me through the darkest and loneliest days.

When I entered therapy, it was great to meet others who were also struggling, to know that I wasn't alone. I had a knack for lifting up others during group therapy. The other patients and I explored media myths, religion, spirituality, intuitive eating, yoga, meditation, and why we felt such hatred toward ourselves. I stayed in the center for twenty-one days. To this day, it remains one of the greatest experiences of my life.

One exercise that we had to do in therapy was go to a restaurant and order off the menu without altering the meal. This meant not putting dressing on the side, not taking off olives, eating only half the bread to cut carbs, etc.—something I certainly wasn't used to doing. I was the queen of having dressing on the side and no cheese, olives, or nuts. There were many times during the height of my disease when I would not eat a meal if the restaurant accidentally put cheese or dressing on the salad when I had asked for it without. For our therapy exercise, we went to a Greek restaurant that only served gyros. Gyros are greasy—and thick with heavy ingredients such as rich meats and lots of cheese and bread. I had never eaten one before! (Well, now I know they are very yummy!) They are almost like a Subway Sub but not as "healthy." I had no idea what to order, but I asked for the gyro, as I was supposed to do. I sat down at the table, stared at it, and sobbed. I was having an anxiety attack. I was scared of what it would do to me. Would I gain ten pounds? Would I be ugly in a few hours? Would my pants be tight? Would anyone like me if I had extra weight on me? Who would I be without anorexia? Yep . . . all true, real feelings inspired by a gyro. The therapists soothed me as I took my first bite. I cried some more. Tears were streaming down my face, dripping so fast that they reached my chest and seemed to go straight to my heart, which ached for love. I just wanted to love myself and feel loved and not feel this deep emotional pain anymore.

So I ate the gyro.

It took me a good forty-five minutes, but I did it. The next activity of the night was to go for dessert. I couldn't believe my ears. I had to eat another fatty, calorie-dense meal! Most people would jump at the chance and, through my recovery, I now see why. It's good to treat yourself. But at that time, I had no choice. This was part of my treatment plan. I ordered a mint chocolate chip ice cream cone. I remember coming home that night and trying on some of my clothes to make sure they still fit. They did. But I was still scared. Would I have to burn the calories I had just eaten in some other way?

After a good night's rest, I woke up feeling fine—not bloated or puffy—and guess what? My pants still zipped up. I had conquered a major fear and felt euphoric over it! This was a giant leap of faith for me, and I was fine. I wasn't fat, ugly, or stupid because of a gyro and an ice cream cone. I was fine! My thighs weren't huge, and my belly wasn't bloated. There was still work to be done, but I knew I was headed to a full recovery.

I left the facility twenty-one days later with a clear mind and a sense of newfound hope. I went to traditional therapy for a few months. It felt great to be loosening the chains of anorexia's hold on my life. I stopped going to therapy after a while. I continued on my healing journey on my own. I read books and blogs about parenting, marriage, spirituality, and rebirth *any chance I got*. I would sit in carpool lines, walk on treadmills, and eat in restaurants alone, studying life, relationships, and spirituality. I felt as though I had been given a second chance to live. I was working hard on healing myself and making tiny bits of progress every day. I could see changes in how others reacted to me. I was, however, still hanging on just a teeny, tiny bit to controlling my weight and feeling worthless. There remained a big change that needed to happen. I needed a giant burst of progress to catapult me into inspired living.

It finally happened.

This book is titled *Your Wide Awakening* because I believe you can experience small awakenings every day (Oprah calls them "aha" moments) where you may hear a quote a different way, see your loved one in a different light, or take a bite of something and not be scared that it is going to make you a hundred pounds heavier! These miniature awakenings are all small steps toward sustainable recovery. I was doing that with talk therapy, joyful moments with my kids, exploring meditation and yoga, self-help books, reading parenting blogs, etc. These smaller awakenings usually lead up to Your Wide Awakening. You stay committed to living a happy life, maybe by pulling away from toxic people, seeking help, remaining positive, managing stress, making healthier food choices, but you still aren't pulling the trigger. You are still holding on to bits and pieces of old wounds. The beautiful thing is that these awakenings are the process. Your eyes start to open, your ears start to listen, you feel as though you are sunshine breaking through the clouds. There will be setbacks; there will be arguments; life still goes on, but it's up to you to keep pushing forward. Recovery is an ongoing effort—a day-to-day intention to become healthy. You are closer to happiness than you were yesterday. You take the small steps to a full recovery.

Your Wide Awakening is an infinite, life-changing decision where you take hold of the steering wheel and redirect your life.

It's looking fear straight in the eye and not backing down.

It's making the decision one day that you are going to change for good and following through with it. It's about digging deep, getting your hands dirty, and working to get them clean! There are no quick fixes! You finally decide that you will dedicate your life to loving *you*. You take on full responsibility for the direction of your life. You choose *living*, not existing! You leave the dead-end job; stop speaking negatively about yourself; you pack your bags and leave the failing relationship; you stop engaging in self-destructive eating behaviors. You forgive, but do not condone, a painful event that occurred in your life. You choose to live free. You get your second chance at life! You free yourself from pain and struggle and commit to celebrating your life each day. The veil is lifted, and you aren't turning back! This book will show you how I did it. You can too. The time has come to redefine your life!

My Wide Awakening happened on a mountaintop six years ago.

Every year since my daughters' births, I have taken a solo retreat somewhere. My husband enjoys these weekends, when he gets to spend one-on-one time with the girls. Many times I have just gotten in the car and drove wherever my car took me. I have been to all kinds of crazy small towns and have talked to the locals in coffee shops, met awesome new people, and stayed in little resorts with my journal, some books, and life's essentials.

This particular year, I went to the Blue Ridge Mountains in Virginia, and there my Wide Awakening occurred. It was almost as though I transcended into a different realm that day and rebirthed into exactly who I am. I had a spiritually transformative experience.

I went that year to a mountainside resort in central Virginia. On that day, I sat down on a large boulder after a long hike, pulled out my blank journal, and began to write. On one side of the page I wrote, "Accomplishments." On the other side, I wrote, "Things I am grateful for." I found that my lists were getting so long that I had to flip the page over and write on the back. I couldn't believe how rich my life was! I had spent so much time worrying about pleasing every person I encountered and being so involved with an eating disorder that I hadn't taken a deep look at my own life. I had to stop to make it to a yoga class on time, so I dusted myself off and hurried down the mountain.

The yoga class was small, set in a tiny studio in the back of the resort's fitness center but, boy, did *big* things happen during that two-hour class. As I moved from one difficult pose to another, I felt my fears about life float out of my body. A transformation was happening right before my eyes. The meditation was long... tears were flowing from my eyes... joyful tears... I was free, free from my own fears and expectations. I felt solely responsible for *me* and only *me*. I realized, finally, that I love *me*! I let go of the inadequacies I felt as a mother. I released the grief I felt about my mom's absence. I fell back in love with me, my spirit, my soul, and the most authentic version of me filled with love and joy!

The discovery I had in the yoga room that morning was that I am solely responsible for my happiness and how I interpret my life's events. I am 100 percent responsible. I let it all go. I surrendered all my pain to the universe.

> *Some people believe holding on and hanging in there are signs of great strength. However, there are times when it takes much more strength to know when to let go and then do it.*
> —Ann Landers

Since then, I have felt that I recovered fully. I'm embracing learning through making mistakes, loving harder, and growing every day. Yoga and meditation have changed my life too. I meditate every morning and sit with myself several times a day and focus on my breath. The tasks, frustrations, and stresses that we all experience each day seem to float in and out of my consciousness. I feel fully prepared to take on whatever heads my way. Yoga has also changed the way I feel about my body.

So I'm here to tell you that whatever you are struggling with—whether it be the loss of a loved one, an eating disorder, depression, bingeing and purging, an unhealthy relationship with food—you can heal yourself! The contents of this book represent over fifteen years of tried-and-true research on my part. It was a long journey of immersing myself in relentless self-improvement, spirituality, yoga, alternative medicine, therapy, books, blogs, journals, magazines, websites solely dedicated to finding one's purpose, and living the healthiest, most joyful, life possible. The journey never stops. Life is not always easy. We can't simply wish for the situation to get better. We have to do some heavy lifting to get where we need to be. I work at keeping a lid on the negative thoughts I have on a daily basis. The work that you do minute-to-minute eventually adds up. Recovery is possible!

Think of me as your guinea pig. I have done the hard work to develop the tools to recovery. Give yourself the gift or give it to someone you know who's struggling right now with exploring what's already inside of them. The following nine chapters of this book will give you the focus to overcome an eating disorder and finally achieve Your Wide Awakening.

> *The joy of life consists in the exercise of one's energies, continual growth, constant change, the enjoyment of every new experience. To stop means simply to die. The eternal mistake of mankind is to set up an attainable ideal.*
> —Aleister Crowley

I

Mind

CHAPTER

1

Why Do We Have Eating Disorders?

In a world full of so much wonder, excitement, and possibility, why are there addictions, diseases, and illnesses in this world? Why are there such things as eating disorders?

Simply stated, we don't believe we are worth it. We believe that we are not good enough.

Fundamentally, the root of all disease is the negative or positive relationship we have with ourselves. At the very bottom layer of addictions, diseases, and ailments is the same symptom of a low sense of self-worth, shame, and the feeling of having been deeply hurt by someone or something. It starts in the mind.

This media-crazed, celebrity-obsessed, and pharmaceutical-numbed world around you wants you to be like it. It wants you to buy its products, join its team, and spend your money! There are all sorts of tricks, temptations, and marketing schemes to get you to buy products or services on impulse. These ads trick us into believing we are never good enough—and such and such product will help us lose weight or make us beautiful. I am not saying that all products and services are bad, but much of the advertising is plain slimy and sick! It sets us up to compare ourselves to other people and make us feel like we don't have it all. We do! We were born with all we need!

Photoshopped images, advertising schemes, and the media's relentless pushing of an unattainable ideal grab us and suck us in at our lowest points! Then we are stuck with a Thigh Master, a cabinet full of diet pills, and the latest diet book collecting dust on our bookshelves. My favorite, the treadmill, is now a clothes hanger. We've all done it. No one is immune.

Some of us, those with the eating disorders, take it a bit further because we have a more fragile temperament. (More about this in chapter 2.) We start engaging in negative self-talk, believing the media hype, and developing an unhealthy relationship with food and our bodies.

The truth is that we are enough already. Our heartbeat is reason enough to know that we are here to live out a purpose and not to conform to what is acceptable for a whole population. A size 0 body is not ideal for the whole population—who are we kidding? The images in the media are mostly unrealistic! Why can't we just strive to feel good in the bodies given to us at birth? What's *our* happy place/space/weight? It's not realistic—and it's simply unhealthy—to take drastic measures to get to a specific size or weight when your body is at peak health at a size 12.

Are you suffering with an eating disorder or an unhealthy relationship with food? Here are some questions you might want to ask yourself or someone you suspect may be struggling:

1. Do you constantly think about food?
2. Do you label some foods as good and bad? For instance, is ice cream off-limits?
3. Do you obsess over specific body parts that you feel are fat?
4. Do you worry often about what you ate and whether you will gain weight after a meal?
5. Do you vomit after eating?
6. Do you binge at least twice a week? For instance, do you eat until you are uncomfortable?
7. Do you exercise compulsively to burn calories?
8. Do you limit your food intake and/or count calories, fat grams, carbohydrate grams, etc.?
9. Do you weigh yourself several times a day?
10. Do you see an overweight person in the mirror even though you are thin?

11. Do you sneak or hide food?
12. Do you follow the media hype of the latest diet trend? Do you start and stop diets regularly?
13. Do you look in the mirror and not like what you see?

When I was at the lowest point of my eating disorder, I answered every question with a yes. If you answered yes to *any* of the questions, this book is for you. It's time to examine what you are seeking and give you the courage to stand up to the negative self-talk and destructive behaviors and conquer them once and for all.

It is also important to acknowledge that you don't have to have a clinically diagnosed eating disorder to have a distorted body image or feel ashamed of your weight. You have to know that you are not living your fullest potential by restricting what you eat, bingeing, purging, overexercising, engaging in mindless eating, or looking in the mirror and not liking what you see.

Why did I suffer?

At the time of my mom's death, I felt numb and lost. So instead of journaling, going to church, going to therapy, focusing on excelling in school, etc. (all healthy coping mechanisms that we will discuss later), I decided to turn my attention to drama. Not the high school play drama—well, I did that too!—but gossiping, staying in unhealthy relationships, going out all day and night, and being rebellious. My inner demons told me that I was not good enough, smart enough, pretty enough, or funny enough. I really cared what people thought of me. If I wasn't perfect, I felt awful. This manifested in my getting into trouble at times and getting average grades. The beautiful thing is that I did have a smidgen of self-respect—and enough fear—not to take heavy drugs or engage in sexual behaviors. Thank heavens! There are so many people in the world who struggle with addictions, bad habits, negative self-talk, etc. We hide our true selves and put on a people-pleasing mask that is downright ugly. I continued the same behaviors all through college.

When I developed anorexia in college, I used it as a way to avoid the difficulties in my life. It was a great distraction from feeling any pain, mostly about my mom's death and my poor opinion of myself. Unhealthy behaviors help people avoid unpleasant, painful emotions. People develop addictions, disorders, or diseases, not only to substances—drugs, alcohol, nicotine, caffeine, sugar, and food—but also to activities, such as gambling, having sex, cutting, surfing the Internet, working, and shopping. I chose to hurt my body.

It was easier to avoid the pain. I had no desire to feel it in order to heal it. I wanted to distract myself with diet books, endless hours of exercise, isolating myself from friends and family, and creating drama in my life. I was never really taught in school or at home how to handle negative feelings and negative thinking. My natural reaction was to fight against the way that I felt. That simply does not work. I see it with my kids. If I don't allow my kids to experience painful emotions, I miss out on important teaching lessons. With methods I will show you here, I teach them ways to handle their thoughts, anxieties, and fears instead of stuffing them down.

When I was anorexic, I was depressed. It was easy to stay home, isolate, and use unhealthy coping mechanisms like controlling my calories, spending lots of time in front of the mirror critiquing my appearance, overexercising, and reading about the latest diet to cope with my feelings of unworthiness. Anorexia is a monster. It's so difficult to tame. I knew I was living a meek life. I was weak until I realized my strength. We all have strength—we are all born with that. Through our experiences, childhood pain, and the efforts of the world to change us, we can lose that strength and succumb to unhealthy coping mechanisms. But you can train your mind to get back your inner strength!

I know it's harder to pursue your dreams because you have to fight through your fears and make mistakes. You have to face criticism. To me, any criticism was downright painful to hear! When I realized that it was the other person's projection of himself or herself, I knew there was nothing wrong with me. The person was projecting feelings of inadequacy onto me, and I took the fall. Things started to change in my world when I realized that it wasn't about me; it was about them.

When you isolate and live in a state of fear, you stay safe and hidden and live a life with no possibility, dreams, and learning. You don't live your true potential.

This is isn't living; it's existing.

It's getting by with the minimum, with no purpose in your days. Happiness lies on the other side of living—making mistakes and facing your fears. Overcoming your fears builds your self-esteem. It builds confidence.

Remember the gyro story? I conquered my fear, and, as a result, I began to believe that recovery was a possibility.

The funny thing is that the more you avoid the issue, the *bigger* it becomes. (Ugh. No, it's not going away. There is no magic wand, no sorcerer granting you three wishes, and no flood that washes the problem away. Darn it!) So, the longer you avoid facing an issue, the *bigger* it becomes and the *harder* it is to break down the emotional wall or fight the disease.

Have you ever skipped a few regular dentist appointments? Well, I have. After the birth of my second daughter, I put most of my medical appointments on hold to fit my girls' schedules. Not a good choice—rather, an excuse!

I do not enjoy the dentist. A year went by, and a back molar started to get sensitive. A few months after that, I was eating popcorn with my family and bit down on a kernel. My back tooth cracked. Yes, cracked! My face got red, I started to sweat, and I realized that part of my tooth had just come off. Yes—off. See ya later, old buddy for twenty years. Gone. I was somewhat embarrassed to call the dentist, so I put it on hold for a few more months. (See where I am going with this, friends?)

I got to the point of saying, "This is *enough!*" I called the local dentist, set up an appointment, and was ready to face my fear of the monstrous drill and the giant, scary needle! I was not putting up with this pain and embarrassment and funky chewing anymore! Well, after two years of not going to the dentist and trying to avoid the issue, I went in. The dentist revealed the fateful news: I needed a root canal.

The good news is that the tooth is fixed with a shiny new crown on it. I have no pain or sensitivity, and I am now back on track with biannual appointments.

The less you listen to your body's whispers (physical aches and pains; the little voice inside that recognizes the right thing to do), the more they turn into shouts—like the flu, root canals (ahem . . .), or worse, tumors. The mind and body are connected, so your body hears every thought you think and every word you say. We develop these aches, pains, colds, etc., as a result of not feeling a traumatic event from our past, not thinking you are [fill in the blank] enough, and experiencing daily stress. Your body stores those thoughts in certain organs, and they become diseased.

I never felt that I was smart enough, pretty enough, or skinny enough and never felt worthy enough to live a happy life. Until I figured out that I needed to heal from my mom's early death and old childhood wounds through intense therapy, forgive many people in my past, and, most of all, forgive myself, I could not experience my soul's wide awakening. I had to get back into my mind.

When I first started to get serious about healing my eating disorder in the late 1990s, I focused on healing myself through eating again. I focused only on the physical side of the eating disorder. I still wasn't making any connection with healing my mind. It was too hard. My thoughts were scattered. I was an emotional wreck, and I had to eat again. I had so much stored anger, resentment, and was living the "why me?" mantra in my head. Why did my mom die so young? Why do I have no friends? Why do I like having this eating disorder? So my head was still playing the same news reel announcing: "I am dumb, I am fat, I am unworthy, I am stupid." So I taught myself how to eat healthfully, but my diet was still restricted. I convinced myself that "I was eating," so I thought I was getting better and could trick the people around me into thinking that I didn't have an eating disorder anymore. My mind never healed. I needed to heal my past traumatic experiences once and for all. Gaining the physical weight helped a little, but my mind needed to be healed. Fixing the body was easy for me; I was putting food in my mouth, but my mind was telling me all these hateful things about myself. You can't just heal the body when you have anorexia because it started in the mind.

Below I present tools (developed through tried-and-true experimentation on yours truly) that will help you to "Feel it to Heal It." This means healing from a past traumatic experience (e.g., being bullied as a child, a death in the family, rape, a car crash, a painful divorce, etc.) Your eating disorder was birthed in the moment when you didn't forgive that experience or let it go. You have carried the weight of it for so long. This is really what your eating addiction and your unhealthy habits and/or disorder stem from. To live the life of your dreams, you have to let all the pain come up so you can heal it. Unresolved problems wreak havoc in your mind and body. It will *never* do you any good to stuff them down with unhealthy methods. Pain can be the catalyst to our transformation/awakening. If we don't listen to the wisdom of the soul (which happens when we busy ourselves with time wasters and mindless activities, and when we listen to others' opinions rather than our own), we will experience the pain repeatedly until we learn the lesson our soul is trying to teach us. Allow yourself, finally, to face your problems Take it from me. It was a long ten years of fighting anorexia.

We are talking big stuff here, people. I am not talking about the argument you just had with your boss or significant other. Those sorts of things happen in day-to-day living. (We will get to ways of dealing with day-to-day stress later!)

We all go through some tough stuff. No one gets through life without some battle scars. Do not avoid painful experiences by stuffing them down with food, lack of food, overexercising, withdrawal, or some other unhealthy coping mechanism. Food is a source of fuel and pleasure, but it is not where you will find fulfillment. Feel it!

I am talking about something you think about that brings you deep emotional pain. The event—a painful circumstance—on which you have put a big Band-Aid but that is still not healing.

Let's begin the process of getting to the bottom of your emotional pain and letting it go, once and for all.

Your Wide-Awake Plan to Heal Emotional Pain

1. *Identify what bothers you.* What's your story? What is the one thing your friends can say they know has deeply hurt you? For instance, it could be divorce, abandonment by a parent(s), death of a loved one, a tough breakup with a friend or boyfriend/girlfriend. What pains you most days? Who hurt you?
2. *Awareness with breath.* Go to a safe place and practice this breathing exercise. Hold the event or person in your heart. Inhale deeply at the count of six, and exhale at the count of four. Do this six times. You will be controlling your breath for a full minute to stimulate the parasympathetic nervous system.

    Biology 101: Your nervous system operates in two different ways. These two aspects of the nervous system are called the sympathetic nervous system and the parasympathetic nervous system. When you have a stressful thought or feeling, your sympathetic nervous system kicks in. You will feel this as your heart racing, your palms sweating, and the emergence of negative emotions like anger, sadness, or—most of all—fear. This is stress! You can't think straight, and you say things you shouldn't say, perhaps regretting it later. It's a major stress response and causes sensory overload. Then the brain makes stress hormones called cortisol, epinephrine, and norepinephrine, which wreak havoc on your body and all its organs.

Your parasympathetic nervous system works in the opposite way. It is stimulated through steady, even breath and centering yourself with positive thoughts and feelings. You want to get into your parasympathetic state as often as possible, especially when you are bringing up old traumas.

Some uncomfortable emotions may come up here. Do not stop what you are doing. Breathe through the pain. Tell yourself you are safe. Give yourself this time to heal. This exercise will change your life if you keep doing it. Do not stop when it gets uncomfortable. You are doing great.

3. *Acknowledge the thought, the hurtful remark, the tragic event, the struggle or disagreement with the person(s).* In your seated position, think about how you must have felt when that terrible stuff happened. How would you speak to that hurt little child or to someone going through the same experience as you? I know you wouldn't put them down and yell at them. So please do not do that to yourself. With all the wisdom you have accumulated to this point in your life, show your inner child love and compassion. Maybe give yourself a hug.

4. *Now, imagine yourself looking in on that hurt child or adult you were when you were experiencing that painful event.* Write a letter to yourself about that moment. Let yourself know that everything is going to be okay and that it was never your fault. Write in the letter to yourself, "It wasn't my fault. I forgive myself. I forgive [insert name]" ten times.

5. *Next, reconceptualize the experience/setback/obstacle as a gift.* After you have felt that initial emotion, recast the experience as part of your journey of self-growth. Everything happens for a reason. The past will never change. It's done. Work at forgiving the experience.

The person who hurt you was really hurting him or herself. He or she wasn't trying to hurt you, but as they say, "Hurt people, hurt people." The person was doing the best he or she could with what he or she knew. You can't control what happened, but you can control how you interpret it. You must also forgive yourself. It may have been something you did and for which you have never forgiven yourself. This is *your* path, and it will be different from that of your best friends, your siblings, or anyone you know. No two paths are alike. It may take days or weeks to work through the pain. We don't want it to turn into months—or worse, years—as it did for me.

6. *Now go move your body for a few minutes.* Stand up, breathe, and move. Take a leisurely walk out in nature. Practice yoga, tai chi, or simple stretching. If you have only five or ten minutes, do a few sets of push-ups, a few sun salutations, or three rounds of jumping jacks. Get back into your body, and let it go. Let the negative thoughts and energy move through you and outside your body. You have been carrying them for too long!

7. *Next, practice self-care by doing what you love.* Do you like to get lost in a book, play board games or cards or do crafts with your kids, take a long bath, spend time with friends, drink your favorite tea or coffee, or listen to your favorite music? Find your healthy pleasure, and do it right now. Your body and mind crave this.

8. *Then, do what I did on the mountaintop that day.* Get out your journal, go to a calm, quiet spot, and draw a line down the page. List all your accomplishments on one side. They can be things as simple as organizing your closet (no small task for me! Ha!), scoring your first goal in soccer as a kid, buying your first car or home, or graduating from high school. On the other side of the page, list all the things/people/events you are grateful for. Add to this list as needed, and keep it on the first pages of your journal. When you reflect on what you are grateful for, you begin to receive more things to be grateful for. Open your journal every morning to remind yourself all that you are and all that you have to be grateful for. Just feeling thankful can turn a dark day into a brighter one. As the great philosopher and author Eckhardt Tolle says, "If the

only prayer you said in your whole life was, 'Thank you,' that would suffice."

9. *If the event is just too big for you to take on yourself, go see a therapist/life coach/priest.* Please! Some pretty bad stuff can happen to us, and it can be difficult to come to terms with, without the help of a professional. Believe me, they have seen all kinds of traumas, so don't think your story is the worst one they've ever heard. You may not be able to break the pain without the help of a therapist. This is money invested in your life. Forget the negative stigma around therapy, which implies that you are "crazy" for going. I have gone to therapy several times over the past twenty years and wouldn't change the experiences and the things I learned about myself for the world.

This is the start of your healing process. The root of your eating disorder lies in that defining experience. Your mind tricked you in that moment into believing that you did not have worth. It's time to start believing in yourself and getting your mind back on track. Be brave in letting go.

This may take some time, but no one is asking for perfection—just progress. You owe it yourself to heal your past and start fresh and new in each moment. Stay present and love yourself deeply for being aware of what you need to deal with.

In the next chapter we will go deeper into beginning to love yourself, with all the bumps, bruises, quirks, and traits that make you exactly who you are. Lovable, wonderful, unique you.

> *To be beautiful means to be yourself. You don't need to be accepted by others. You need to accept yourself.*
> –Thich Nhat Hanh

CHAPTER

2

Nature vs. Nurture

> *Nature, we are starting to realize, is every bit as important as nurture. Genetic influences, brain chemistry, and neurological development contribute strongly to who we are as children and what we become as adults. For example, tendencies to excessive worrying or timidity, leadership qualities, risk-taking, obedience to authority, all appear to have a constitutional aspect.*
>
> –Stanley Turecki

Whether we like it or not, we are born with a certain temperament. No two persons are exactly alike. Generally, temperament is identified with personality components that are biological rather than learned. It's a style of behavior, and it's relatively consistent across situations and age spans. We are all different in how we take in information through our five senses, how we react to the environment with certain levels of intensity, and how we regulate our stress levels. Our temperament includes traits such as level of activity, adaptability, intensity, distractibility, sensory threshold (for example, what may be too loud for one person may be quiet to another), and mood.

It's important to bring this up because, instead of fighting our inherent nature, we must work with it.

In the book, *The Temperamental Thread*, Dana Press likens differing temperaments to different breeds of dogs. A pit bull has a different temperament than a poodle because the biology of their brains is completely different. When a tragic event or stressful situation pops up in our lives, it is our temperament that determines how we will react to it. Some may throw a temper tantrum, withdraw, internalize, and generally cope with unhealthy means. Others may be more laid-back, take it as it comes, and move through it and with it, not against it. These types of people are less likely to develop addictions, disorders, or illnesses. Their stress levels are not as high, and they take things in stride. They move on quickly, rather than sulking after the stressful event.

Neither reaction or temperament is good or bad; it is what it is. What is more important is that your temperament can be adjusted through experience. You *can* teach an old dog new tricks. This is where the nurture argument can be brought up. Nurture is how you were raised, and the experiences you have had to this point determine who you are. In my opinion, nature and nurture come together to produce your personality. There is still great debate in the psychology world whether one is more important than the other, but I will leave that for you to research.

If you are like me, I had to learn how to stop throwing temper tantrums, manage my stressful emotions in a calming way, and to break the cycle of beating myself up over a mistake, a painful event, an accident, or a bad choice. I would beat myself up for weeks!

You can liken it to parenting. Say, you have three children. No two people are the same—we are all hard-wired differently—so you need to adjust your approach, parenting each child according to his or her temperament. Tough, I know, but it's the only way you will avoid power struggles and ensure some level of success for each child.

This principle also applies if you are the boss at work. You are going to motivate and treat each colleague or employee a little differently. What makes one tick may not work for the other one.

Finally, I will use Oprah Winfrey as an another great example of the nature versus nurture debate. She was brought up in Mississippi by her grandmother in her early childhood. At age seven, she moved to Milwaukee to live with her mother. When she was nine years old, she was raped. At ten years old, she was molested by her cousin's boyfriend and her uncle. When she was fourteen, she ran away from home and became pregnant. She hid the pregnancy until the day the child was born. The child died soon after its birth.

Winfrey's temperament was to adapt, change, grow, heal. She was born with a self-assuredness that helped her adapt to many situations. In a documentary of her life, she proclaims that all that tragedy just gave her strength to say, "I'll show them!"

Another person, with a sensitive or fragile temperament, might have reacted to this early tragedy by withdrawing, becoming introverted or shy, abusing him or herself with alcohol or drugs, or developing an eating disorder.

I am here to tell you that you are not your biology or your circumstances. You are not "just born that way," and it is not true that "that event made me who I am." You are both, but you need to understand the core of who you really are and accept it unapologetically.

Chances are, if you are reading this book, you may exhibit some of the traits of a highly sensitive person, or there is someone close to you who does. In her groundbreaking book, *The Highly Sensitive Person*, Dr. Elaine Aron reveals that this trait exists in 20 percent of the population. According to Dr. Aron's definition, the Highly Sensitive Person (HSP) has a sensitive nervous system, is aware of small things in his or her surroundings, is more easily overwhelmed in a highly stimulating environment, and has a difficult time managing stressful situations. Dr. Aron has a great self-test on her website, www.hsperson.com, that reveals whether you fit the description. According to Dr. Aron, a Highly Sensitive person:

- is overstimulated easily
- is extremely creative
- is cautious and thinks before doing
- is sensitive to loud noises, tight clothing, and strong sense of smells and tastes, and dislikes clutter and chaos
- needs order
- has a hard time saying no to others' requests
- is very empathetic to others, feels their pain, and tries to help—sometimes to a fault
- is a deep thinker, a soul searcher

- is uncomfortable when things get out of control
- shows concern and worries about many things
- has deep respect for music, nature, and art

Do you or does someone you love have any of these traits?

The wonderful thing about having these traits is that some of the greatest achievers of our time had these traits too. People like Albert Einstein, Abraham Lincoln, Martin Luther King, Jr., Princess Diana, Mother Teresa, and Walt Disney, all exhibited some of these characteristics. They were able to embrace and accept their temperament and give back to the world in very big ways. You can too!

To live a rich, fulfilling life, you must not try to change anything about yourself. When you fully embrace all that you already are and recognize that you are enough as is, then your insecurities will vanish. Celebrate your traits. Work with them. You were born with these gifts. They offer endless possibilities for your life. You can give back to the world in ways that fulfill you and many other people.

When I was suffering from anorexia, I took personally every remark, grimace, or careless action. I internalized it all the way down to my core. I am quite obviously a highly sensitive person. What I didn't realize was that the remark, grimace, or action was not my issue. It was the result of the other person in the room dealing with his or her own "stuff." My nervous system is so sensitive that I internalized every such remark or gesture as though it were prompted by something I had said or done that must have upset them! This, of course, was just not true.

After my first daughter was born, I attended to every sound, cry, or whimper because I felt like it was my fault that she was crying. Of course, you must do your best job as a mother to console and nurture a little baby, but I was overdoing it and wearing myself out. Crying is a baby's only form of communication. Usually, it is brought on by some form of overstimulation; they need to express that energy loudly—and now! It has nothing to do with your parenting.

Can you identify that you were born with a certain temperament? You are stronger than you ever imagined because of all you have been through. Your sensitivity has brought you through really tough times that have allowed you to grow into the person you are today.

This book will show you that there is nothing you need to change about who you are. The strategies and information I provide here are just healthy tweaks and tried-and-true coping mechanisms that I have used to make life easier. Instead of beating yourself up over the fact that you "feel" a bit more, are more likely to let someone use you or hurt you, or that you made a mistake, you will learn to forgive yourself, forgive others and let go of resentment, and experience the rebirth of self-love, happiness, and bliss that you so deserve. Don't fight who you are; be who you are!

Wide-Awake Reflection

In your journal, write down all your strengths. Some examples are: you are a good listener, a great artist; you are compassionate and maybe you make people laugh. Make a list and embrace those strengths. Can you start sharing them with at least one person today? Also, think back to a time when you were free of judging yourself, free of any harmful behaviors—a joyful period in your life. What were you doing? Do you picture yourself laughing on the playground or cuddling with your mother? Try to capture that moment in your mind. That is the essence of who you are. Play up your strengths. Seek work and relationships that complement who you really are. Drown out the noise of the TV, the Internet, and the radio telling you that you should be something else. Really explore what you love about you.

> *The principle of all successful effort is to try to do not what is absolutely the best, but what is easily within our power, and suited for our temperament and condition.*
> –John Ruskin

CHAPTER

3

Self-Love

I am sure you have heard someone tell you, you must love yourself first. Sounds so easy, right? Wrong! The root of most of our emotional pain is our lack of self-love. It took me a long time—over twenty-five years—to understand that. I used to think loving yourself was cocky, arrogant, boastful, and unbecoming. I thought people who exhibited self-love were all about themselves—selfish, insincere, and rude. But there is a major difference between loving oneself and being narcissistic or self-obsessed!

Loving yourself is accepting yourself for what you enjoy and what you love; it is loving your body and loving your "flaws" too. We live in a celebrity—and media-obsessed society where someone is always trying to sell you a product or service you must have, trying to make you rethink your inner truths, and/or selling you a mocked up/photoshopped fantasy of what you are supposed to look like and how you are supposed to behave. We have also been influenced by our upbringing. Someone close to you may have criticized you for the things you enjoy or told you a specific way to behave and may have rejected you for not behaving the way they wanted you to. You changed for them and thus were not expressing your authentic self. Expressing one's authentic self without needing anyone's approval is the basis of self-love.

Have you ever been part of a photo shoot or had your family picture taken? How many pictures did you take to get that perfect shot? Well, in the media world, first the subject gets his or her makeup done to even skin tone and highlight lips, eyes, and cheeks. Then the photographer takes hundreds of pictures to get that one perfect cover shot. Next, the image is sent to editing, where they photoshop, nip, tuck, highlight, and "clean up" the image and finally print on glossy paper. The cover is complete! Yes, after all of that! It's a mocked-up, insincere version of reality.

Let's take actors and actresses who are getting ready for the Oscars or some other big awards show. They usually start preparing for the event at least three weeks prior with facial and body treatments, cosmetic enhancements, strict diets, and grueling workout regimens. They are sent dresses to try on by the best fashion designers in the world. Alterations are then begun to ensure the best fit after the best dress has been chosen. As the event draws closer, tanning begins, more alterations are made, and the dream team of hair mavens, makeup gurus and personal stylists is assembled. They are set to arrive at least eight hours before red-carpet arrival time. The work begins in the morning with a workout and light eating throughout the day. Hair can take an hour or more. Makeup too! Jewelry, shoes, purse, undergarments (Spanx, anyone?) are lined up and perfectly chosen to accessorize the look. Then showtime! Wow. Are you tired? And *this* is the image we compare ourselves to? Not anymore.

This image is not reality, as you can see. I remember as a young girl reading many issues of *Seventeen* magazine, wanting to be a model. Dreaming of shining red lips that weren't chapped, a mole placed on that "perfect" spot on my face. Oh, and the fashion . . . but doesn't she look so happy wearing that polka-dotted skirt with the striped blouse and hot-pink blazer and shiny patent leather neon-pink stilettos! Oh, and the gobs of jewelry! It's all fantasy, and, as young impressionable minds will do, we believed it was real.

We must dispel the myth that these models roll out of bed looking the way they do. Yes, they may have more symmetrical faces than most, and their limbs are longer than those of 99.9 percent of us, so the clothes drape on them as though they were on a hanger. You were not born with those traits, and that's okay. Models are models because they have those traits. The corporate giants of this world trick us into believing that we are not enough.

You were born a lawyer, a nurse, an accountant, a teacher, a stay-at-home mom, a nail technician, not a model! Yes, you can love yourself for all that you are! There is no other person with your DNA, your fingerprints, those freckles in the same pattern, and the same life experiences you have had. You are *you*! There is no one better, worse, or the same as you. You are unique. You matter.

Part of the your healing journey requires you to return to Love. Kick that negative chatter to the curb and begin to embrace your inner and outer beauty. When you feel yourself engaging in negative self-talk or purging or picking at your skin folds, recenter your thoughts to self-love.

There are many methods for quieting that chatter and getting back to loving yourself. These are some helpful methods I have developed on my journey to practicing self-love.

1. Affirmations

One of my favorite movies is the movie *The Help* (2011). The movie revolves around a group of African-American maids who collaborate with a young white girl to write a book about how African-Americans were treated in the early 1900s. One of the African-American women (Abilene) is a maid and a nanny to a young toddler. The mother of the young girl is cold, brazen, and unkind to the maid, to her husband, and most of all, to her young daughter. The maid takes on the role of being the girl's mother by doing the necessary things such as potty training; feeding; reading her books; and giving her love, attention, and affection, etc. Throughout the movie, she is constantly reminding the little girl of the following three things:

"You is kind. You is smart. And you is important."

Broken English. Yes. Yet so profound.

I went to see the movie twice in the theaters. I bawled my eyes out during the scenes in which this line was repeated. The story unfolds beautifully as Abilene practices what she preaches, moving on from being a maid at the end of the movie—realizing her worth and not looking back. She leaves the young girl behind, but leaves her a legacy with those three affirmations and her early influence. Abilene has no idea where she is going, but to me her faith is strong, and she knows that everything will work out in the end, as it always does.

You may have a tape that plays negative self-talk repeatedly in your head. You may have had someone tell you that you weren't beautiful, you weren't smart, that you don't matter, etc. As a child, name calling may have stung and stayed with you.

Whoever told you these things, silently say to yourself, "Thank you." They taught you that this was a reflection of what they felt about *themselves*, not about you. Forgive them and show them compassion. Remember, hurt people hurt people. Thank them for showing you what not to be or say.

Now, back to that nasty, negative self-talk you keep repeating to yourself every day. Louise Hay, author of many self-help books, publisher, cancer survivor, philanthropist, and pioneer of positive thinking is the Queen of Affirmations. She believes your thoughts can change your world.

In her book *You Can Heal Your Life*, she asserts that an affirmation is "something you say to yourself that you believe to be true." It can be a positive or negative statement you say or think about yourself. Some of your affirmations may be, "I am so fat" or "I am so ugly" or "I am so stupid." If we are responsible for all the choices we make in our lives, we must be responsible for the thoughts that we think in our lives too. A little trick Hay and one of my therapists taught me when you are thinking negative thoughts is to:

(a) hear the thought. You have complete control over your thoughts, not your emotions;
(b) acknowledge it, and say something like, "Oh, that's nice";
(c) change the thought to, "I am kind," for example, or "I have nice shoulders" or "All is well" or "My smile is pretty." This can be done while looking at yourself in the mirror, deep into your eyes, with a gaze and a glow that you would give to your own child or any other child you may know and care for deeply. It is also helpful to approach yourself as if you were talking to a younger version of you;
(d) have a few statements that you know are true about you that you believe with all your heart. In an anorexic's mind, it may be hard to find one or two things, but do your very best. When you wake up in the morning, before you walk into work or to school, and when you go to bed, repeat your positive affirmation to yourself. An example

might be, "I'm a thoughtful person, and I love that about me." Tell yourself you are doing the best you can, always. Affirming who you are with loving thoughts and words is a wonderful act of self-love. Commit to changing your negative thoughts when you hear them and choose a more loving thought. Another helpful thing I do is wear specific jewelry with spiritual messages and bracelets that remind me to stay calm and positive. When I notice that I am using a negative affirmation like "I am stupid" or "I am a bad person," I look at the necklace, and instantly it can bring me back to the present.

Many of us live in a state of gloom and doom for so long because we often use the words "I am" with a negative thought. Many say all kinds of nasty things like fat, dumb, ugly, not worthy. It is important to reframe your thoughts to: "I am smart, funny, pretty," etc. You don't have to believe it at the time. Practice it every day and your unconscious will start to believe it. Use the above exercise when you catch yourself saying unkind things to yourself. The criticizing needs to stop now. You are enough as is. Forgive yourself for not being perfect. Nobody is.

Your world is a reflection of the constant thoughts you think. Choose the good ones.

2. Stay present.

Our brains work on autopilot most of the time. We jump from thought to thought, minute by minute. "What should I make for dinner tonight? I have to pick up a gift for my friend. I have to check my inbox. I can't believe he said that to me yesterday. Has the mail carrier come yet? What time is it? How long is this gonna take?" Blah. Blah. Blah. All these questions relate to things happening in the past or the future, not in the now. Stay focused on what you are doing in this moment. Worrying about the future or living in the past are rotten places to live. You are either worrying about what may or may not happen, wishing things could be different in your past, or wishing the present was like the past. A self-loving thing to do is to stay present. Live in the moment. Now. This moment is all we have.

3. Forgive Yourself and Others

I remember when I was in the midst of fighting anorexia, many family members, friends, and therapists urged me to start eating, get out of bed, and live. The truth was that I saw no point. I was not taking in what they had to say about me (i.e., you are smart, pretty, funny, etc.) and *listening*. They were all happy and busy with their own lives, and I felt nothing. I felt that I added no value to the world around me. I was stuck. I was ungrateful for the gift of life.

Steadily, I started to become more willing to change my life. That only happened through learning to forgive myself for things that had happened in the past and for others' mistakes. The ultimate gift of self-love is to forgive yourself for your mistakes. Everybody makes mistakes. It's important to know that. Forgiving yourself for the ones you have made will change your life.

When my girls were born, I saw their joy for life, their unconditional love, and their smiles, which filled a room. When I started to use their attitudes about their young lives as role models, mine started to shift. They make mistakes every day. They get into things they shouldn't. They fall down numerous times before they learn to walk. Every time they fall, they stand back up until they learn to walk!

Have you ever noticed a baby's willingness to try new things?

They are little explorers getting into drawers, flipping light switches, trying new foods (well, some!), climbing stairs, learning to ride a bike... the list goes on. These lively young souls learn something new each day and take chances one small shift at a time. They don't stop to beat themselves up that they just stumbled and didn't walk the first try. They don't quit. They keep making small improvements each day. That is what recovery is. Baby steps until you finally walk. Then you run! Then you fly!

As adults, most of us stop renewing and learning, and we get in our own way! Most likely because we forget to forgive ourselves for our mistakes, are pretending to be something we are not, quit trying because of the fear of making another mistake, or neglected to forgive others for theirs along the way.

During your recovery, you may beat yourself up over setbacks. You may feel yourself wanting to restrict, binge, purge, or hurt yourself. When you are experiencing these types of negative thoughts toward yourself or another, it is helpful to take a time-out, a step back from the situation, and to take some time alone.

(a) Go to a peaceful, serene spot where you feel most calm. It must be quiet and free of clutter.
(b) Close your eyes and get into a comfortable, seated position. Take six deep breaths, with a count of six seconds on the inhale through the nose and four seconds on the exhale out of the mouth. Deep breathing for a total of a minute should help you quiet the mind and calm the body.
(c) Focus on whom/what you need to forgive. It can be yourself or a loved one. It can be an event, an argument, or a mistake that happened. What is ailing you today? What are you holding on to? What did that person say to you that you just can't seem to get over/forgive? Did you restrict calories today? Do you binge or purge? Send love and compassion and most of all, forgiveness to yourself or the something or someone who may have hurt you today. They need your love more than anyone. Surrender it and watch it pass in front of you and out into the universe. Be free.
(d) Take a big deep breath. A six-count inhale through the nose and a four-count exhale out of the mouth. Let it go.

You just completed a meditation! We will get deeper into meditation in chapter 8, but this is a focused start. When things come up for you—wanting to restrict food or go running for too long, for example, give yourself just five minutes of self-love. Keep at this meditation, and I promise things will shift. Forgiveness heals. Setbacks make you stronger. It might not feel like that at the time, but keep on going. You are doing great.

Forgiveness unlocks the doors to a happier, healthier life. When we are stuck in resentment, we lose sight of the wonderful things around us and aren't willing to listen, to change, to grow, or to heal.

One of my favorite quotes about forgiveness is from Dodinsky: "Forgive. It doesn't erase their crime, but why should you do the time? Let go of resentment."

You may not like what that person did and certainly you don't excuse their behavior, but it is important to let it go. You don't have to continue a relationship with them, and you never have to trust them again. But don't focus so much on people like that anymore. Focus on the ones who love you. *A Course in Miracles* also states that all forgiveness is a gift you give to yourself. If you can train yourself not to approve of the misdoing but to let it go and have compassion for the hurt soul, you can be free of the control that event or person has over you.

Once you are free of resentment, you can unlock the power of gratitude and then willingness to listen to yourself and others becomes easier. Now your best self can emerge.

4. Gratitude

When I was little, I was often called a "grouch." I think I know why. I was not grateful for anything. Some might say that I was a spoiled brat and would try to manipulate my way into getting what I wanted through pouting, whining, and—my favorite—breaking things, including my eyeglasses.

Yes, I would break my eyeglasses if I did not get my way. What an expensive habit!

Sometimes as adults we have temper tantrums. You know what that looks like: stomping your feet, slamming doors, punching walls, raising your voice, whining, crying, etc. I believe that when the temper tantrums are rare, we began to mature, take life as it is, and move on with solutions rather than focusing on the problems. You become more emotionally mature and aware of your behaviors. You refocus on who you really are, which is love.

That's when we can make gratitude our biggest asset.

When you express gratitude for the struggles *and* the joys, you can be at peace.

What are some ways to bring more gratitude into your life?

(a) Let loved ones know you appreciate them! Sometimes we go through our days not showing how much we care for someone. Write the person a loving note, card, text, or e-mail expressing how much they mean to you. Bring them a small gift that shows you care. Flowers, a card, or a small token of appreciation can go a long way.

(b) Forgive someone. Yes, this again! Anger, bitterness, and resentment block the flow of gratitude. Bless the ones who hurt you. Know that it's their issue that caused them to do wrong to you. They need your forgiveness the most.

(c) Practice a random of act of kindness. Let someone in front of you in traffic. Pay for the toll of the person behind you. Make a meal for the sick, hungry, or poor. Bake cookies for your neighbor.

(d) Write down a list of all *your* wonderful qualities. Put it out there in the universe. You are here for a reason, and it's these qualities of yours that bring light to the world.

(e) Practice gratitude on the hour. Each time an hour ticks by, remember to focus on the good in your life. Focus on what is in front of you. The car you are driving, the computer you own, the pretty smile you have, the glowing eyes, and, most important your beautiful soul.

(f) Reflect on all the wonderful things you have right now in your life. Speak softly to yourself and reflect on all the abundance you have in your life. Make a mental list of all the things and people you are grateful for. Express sincere gratitude.

When you are grateful, fear disappears and abundance appears.
–Tony Robbins

If you let go a little you will have a little peace; if you let go a lot you will have a lot of peace; if you let go completely you will have complete peace.
–Ajahn Chah

5. Pity-Party Intervention

Put those Michael Bolton ballads, wads of Kleenex, and ice cream quarts away. We are having a Pity-Party Intervention!

Looking back on my high school and college days, I was the queen party planner for pity parties. I would sit in my car, blast Celine Dion, and cry for hours that my heart was broken. I would cry if I failed a test or got yelled at by a teacher or a friend. I was dramatic and would wallow in my sorrows—misunderstandings between friends, dating dramas, and any stress that life threw at me—for days and weeks. I would complain, throw my fists up in anger, and have a hissy fit if things did not go as planned.

Well, isn't that how life goes?

Fear ruled my life. I believed that things never went as planned and that I was doomed. What a sad way to look at this gift of life! Have you ever heard the expression "go with the flow"? I scoffed at that expression.

As I started to mature and grow into a young woman after getting a real job upon graduating from college, I started to begin softening my dramatics. I became aware of this (quite frankly) childish, immature behavior. Choosing to handle things maturely is a big step in healing your eating disorder.

Awareness of this behavior is the first step in the right direction. A small step forward is better than no step at all. Some days are better than others. Pity parties should not last days, weeks, or more. After all, you have a grand life to experience!

Have you ever let a misunderstanding or argument spend more than twenty minutes in your head? We often get so involved in our emotional states and moods that we forget who we are. If you have spent far too much time on some issue, it's time for a pity-party intervention. Let it go. Exchange apologies. Shit happens. Don't bring it up again or think about it any longer. This is a tricky one for me, but this is the work I continue to do, so I don't beat myself up over the mistake too often, as I did in the past.

There are problem-solving tools that you can use on a daily basis to handle stress. These tools are similar to what we talked about in chapter 1. They should be used to ease day-to-day stressors and not in a traumatic circumstance.

(a) Breathe. Get back into your body, and take long, deep, controlled breaths to slow the heart rate down. Psychologist John Gottmann, author of *What Makes Love Last?* calls this emotional flooding. When your heart beats ninety to one hundred beats per minute, your body believes there is something chasing you, like a giant bear! It's a natural biological reaction to have this stress response when your heart is signaling to the rest of your body that you are in danger. Yes, your body fights to keep you alive, and something as simple as a car cutting in front of you in traffic (not a bear!) can set off the body's central alarm system. When you experience a stress response, you have entered the sympathetic nervous system zone! Adrenaline, a hormone that protects us during stressful situations, is instantly released into your bloodstream. According to Gottman, it takes twenty minutes for this flooding to pass. "Flooding is a 'biochemical flood' preparing your body for action. The chemicals in your body called neurotransmitters must pass through the neural synapse, be absorbed into the tissues, and passed into the urine before heart rate returns to normal." Bottom line: take twenty minutes away from the situation, breathe, cry, punch a pillow, and let it pass. Let your heart rate come down and your body, mind, and spirit get recentered. It really is the only choice you have at this emotional crossroad. The goal is to switch off the sympathetic nervous system by centering yourself with positive thoughts and feelings.

Once the twenty minutes have passed, start a dialogue with yourself. Talk to other parts of you, not the ego. When your stress levels have escalated during the emotional event, practice saying to yourself, "Even though I am experiencing this feeling, I love and appreciate myself." Give all the love you can muster back to yourself. Tell your loved ones you need some time to cool off. This is so important and key. You deserve that love and attention. Each and every one of us has an inner healer, inner cheerleader, inner hero, inner lover, and inner giver. Use your affirmations, forgive yourself and the party involved, and come back to living and extend your love. Pity Party over!

(b) Pack your bags. Bon voyage! Pat yourself on the back and give yourself a break. Failure to take regular vacations has been associated with early death. The recovery process has been difficult, so get out and enjoy the sunshine and relax. You deserve a break from stress; your body will thank you! Get your down time and some rest and relaxation. Take a trip to a local resort, nearby beach, river or lake, or go explore somewhere you have never been before. You don't have to fly to Tahiti. Just go, relax, unwind, and give yourself a well-deserved break! This is an amazing practice of self-love to reward your hard work in recovery. Call the mother-in-law, get a sitter, or even try a stay-cation (where you stay home and do not engage in any chores, bill paying, etc.; just order out and watch romantic comedies—or at least that's my idea!).

(c) Pick up a book. One of my favorite quotes is by Dr. Seuss. "The more that you read, the more things you will know. The more that you learn, the more places you'll go." Pick up as many books as you can about anorexia recovery, self-help, personal development, or healing. Search the Internet for blogs, Facebook pages, articles on healing. The more you know, the better chance you have of a full recovery. Reading is a self-loving activity because it gives you knowledge and insight nobody can ever take away from you. Read something enlightening every day.

(d) Serve others: A surefire way to nurture self-love is to give to someone else. It's virtually impossible to be sad at the same time you are helping another person. Channel your gifts and bring them to other people. Go help someone who needs your special gifts. (We will talk more about finding and applying your unique gifts in chapter 9.) This will show you that your existence matters to at least one person.

(e) Tapping—EFT (Emotional Freedom Technique)—is a psychological acupressure technique that uses your fingers to stimulate the body's natural healing ability by tapping your body's meridian points while using affirmations. I could write a whole book on this, but many have already done this. (To learn more about Tapping, check out Nick Ortner's book *The Tapping Solution*.) This technique has been used for over five thousand years. This technique combines Chinese acupuncture and modern psychology. It is making headlines in the West to help with emotional baggage such as painful events, anxiety, addictions, eating disorders, etc. It's similar to acupuncture in that it touches specific meridians in your body at your head and chest. Acupuncture is traditionally performed with needles in an office or spa. Acupuncture is definitely beneficial and has many advantages, but it's great that EFT can be done in your own home and by you. It can't get any easier or better than this! In EFT you use your fingers (not needles, yay!) to tap specific points on the body in a repetitious manner while using positive affirmations. It is also painless, and it's easy to perform on yourself. The good news is that this can help you heal yourself and tap into your body's own energy!

When I started doing Tapping, I felt sort of strange, and it seemed highly unlikely that I was going to get anywhere doing it. Then I started researching it. Many famous healers and philosophers I follow were promoting it. Louise Hay was promoting it because it reinforces her belief in using affirmations. I kept at it, and emotional blocks began to soften, and old emotional stuff began to heal.

There are nine different meridian points on your body that you will be tapping. You are to focus on the negative, fear-based emotion that you are feeling presently. Hold the thought in your head as you repeat the following phrase—"Even though I feel _____, I deeply and completely accept myself"—as you are tapping. For this example, you could say, "Even though I feel depressed, I deeply and completely accept myself." Do not say "fat" here, because "fat" is not an emotion. Try to look for the emotion that is hiding. You may feel unworthy, you may feel lonely, you may feel scared. Name the emotion.

Remove any eyeglasses, watches, or jewelry from your body. Start out by placing your index finger and your middle finger on both hands at the top of your head at the center of the skull. You will be using your fingertips, not your finger pads, unless you have very long nails, and then I suggest that you use your finger pads.

a. Tap five to seven times on the top of your head.
b. Next, move down to the start of your eyebrows, close to your nose. Tap five to seven times.
c. Then tap at the corner of the eye.
d. Next, tap gently at the bone under the eye.
e. Now, tap at the area under your nose, above your upper lip.
f. Next, tap about one inch below your clavicle, on your collarbone.
g. Then, tap gently at the sides of the body, about four inches below the armpit.
h. Finally, tap inside your wrists with your fingertips.

You can complete as many rounds as you wish. Check in after each round to see how you are feeling emotionally. Make sure you are repeating the affirmation above as you are tapping. Are you still feeling anxiety, stress, or worry about this specific circumstance? Go for another round until the feelings subside. Accepting yourself, and everything you are feeling, is very healing. All emotions are valid.

The magical effect EFT has had on many has been astounding. It helps you deeply and completely accept the emotions you are having. The emotion is neither good nor bad, but simply what is. There is no judgment on what you are feeling—only acceptance. You are acknowledging the fear rather than denying it. There is a great amount of freedom that comes with acceptance. Acceptance also happens to be the best friend of self-love. Accepting your past and accepting yourself, flaws and all, are very important pieces of recovery.

These are some ways to give yourself the love you deserve. If you don't love yourself, who will?

You are a loving, divine human being. You are not just your flaws, bumps, and bruises; you are also laughter, joy, hope, healing, favorite movies, silly expressions. There are people who love you, and there are people whom you love. Try some of these techniques if you are struggling with doubts or fears or wallowing in self-pity about not being enough. I promise, you will get there. Give yourself time. We are all works in progress. We are here to grow and learn. If we stop growing and learning, we are either six feet under or living a life of misery. It's your choice. Get back to loving you.

Wide-Awake Reflection

Pull out your journal and write down at least twenty "I am" statements. Choose only the positive things you feel about yourself. For example, "I am healthy," "I am nice," "I am friendly." Use the power of the phrase "I am" to boost your self-confidence and focus your energies on your positive traits. Other affirmations can even be things about which you have hopes and dreams that you would like to put out into the universe. For example, "I am a best-selling author." Not true at the moment for me, but I hope to accomplish this one day. Dare to dream your wildest dreams. Refer to these

"I am" statements daily to remind yourself who you really are. Begin, and continue to love yourself exactly as you are.

> *We can complain because rose bushes have thorns or rejoice because thorn bushes have roses.*
> —Abraham Lincoln

II
Body

CHAPTER

4

Wide-Awake Eating

Let food be thy medicine and medicine be thy food.
—Hippocrates

We have worked through a traumatic experience in chapter 1. We have learned some coping strategies to deal with stress. In chapter 3, we learned how to practice self-love. Your eating disorder recovery must start with the mind before we tackle the body. Many therapies start with refeeding or trying to fix the body first. This usually backfires because they haven't dealt with the emotional root of the eating disorder. My eating habits never got corrected until I practiced self-love and self-compassion. I was more open to eating when I began to love myself.

I can understand how it might be difficult to take healthy eating advice from someone who had an eating disorder. When I tell you this, you need to hear me out. I have spent the last fifteen years trying to figure out how to eat healthily. Unlike alcoholics or drug addicts, who don't need to expose themselves to their poison of choice every day, anorexics do need to eat, and the self-denial of food—the control—is the drug. In my recovery, I had to reintroduce things that were wild and crazy to me like corn (yes, the vegetable!), ice cream, meat, foods prepared by others, etc. I would shake like a leaf if a meal was put in front of me because I was afraid I would turn into a big, fat blob if I ate it. This meal would set me further back. Thanksgiving was a disaster for years. Turkey was served with fatty gravy, buttery stuffing, creamed corn, creamed spinach, potatoes (ahhh, carbs!), and rich desserts. I had to face each meal every day with the hope of recovery. There were many hard days, even many hard years. I have done the deep, hard work to get on top. Through trial and error, I discovered my own unique way of eating, and you can figure out yours too! It's already within you; it's your body's set point, unique to you, and only you!

I don't believe in a one-size-fits-all approach to healthy eating. You have to choose what works for you—emotionally, spiritually, and physically.

Wide-Awake Eating

I will never forget my twenty-first birthday, which fell in the summer, during the peak of my anorexic years. My family and friends were meeting me at a restaurant after work to celebrate. I remember driving there, thinking, "What can I eat?" They would all be watching. The anxiety was powerful and painful. I am sure I ordered a salad with nothing on it. No cheese, avocado, nuts, dressing, etc. Anything that had fat in it was off-limits. I was turning twenty-one in the late nineties when the "fat-free" marketing scam was at its height. So all fat was off-limits. At that time, I weighed under one hundred pounds, I had lost quite a bit of hair, my skin was flaking off, my arms had developed a fresh layer of fine, blonde hair, and my mind was cluttered and disorganized. I ended up drinking a lot of alcohol that night, as most do on their twenty-first birthdays, and passing out on my friend's lawn and puking my lettuce and tomatoes (sorry for the visual!) all over her front yard.

As I began to recover the following fall of my senior year in college, I knew I needed to eat to live but wondered how could I eat without gaining weight. I wasn't restricting food as much, but I was controlling the types of foods I ate. I divided food into good and bad categories. So I continued to eat "fat-free" foods, but more of them. I bought sourdough pretzels, ate many bread rolls, fat-free soups, fat-free hot chocolate, etc. Sure, the weight was coming back on, but my head was still playing the mind game of fear and control by limiting my foods to only fat-free items. I was still anorexic, but you wouldn't have known by looking at me. I was at a healthy weight for my height.

When I graduated from college, I was at a healthy weight, and I started my first professional job. At that time, the food-marketing giants had switched their focus to the Atkins Diet. The Atkins Diet claimed that by eating high amounts of protein and fat and very few carbs, you could lose a lot of weight. So here I was again, eating lots of chicken, salmon, turkey, hot dogs without the bun, and egg whites with no bread, rice, potatoes, etc. I did lose weight and maintained a lean physique for a few years doing that, but if a plate of mashed potatoes crossed my path, I would reject it. Yes, the anorexic mind was still present, and it was roaring.

After I got married, I turned to fitness to control my weight. I read the fitness magazines religiously, and they told you when to work out, what to eat, and what weights to lift. My body changed dramatically. My muscles were getting stronger and were popping out everywhere! I liked it a lot. Again, my feelings of unworthiness and lack of confidence were dependent upon what my body looked like and the foods I was consuming. I competed in fitness competitions after the birth of my daughters and loved the feeling of controlling my every meal and my every workout. Here I was, still playing games with anorexia after thirteen years! After my second fitness competition, I got the dreadful news at the doctor's office that my thyroid was not functioning properly. As Oprah Winfrey states, "God was not whispering anymore he was shouting." My body was starting to break down. It was weakened by the overexercising, the strict eating, and the constant critique of its outer appearance. It was time to make another shift in the way I was eating, and I was finally ready. There's nothing like getting bad news at the doctor's office to force you to wake up and change your bad habits.

Your Wide-Awake Way of Eating comes from trial and error. No two bodies are alike. We are all made up of different thoughts, systems, metabolisms, energies, and purposes. I have watched friends eat a whole platter of nachos and not gain a single pound. I have seen family members eat two cookies and pack on the pounds.

You cannot go a week without eating, or your health will suffer dire consequences. Your body starts to break down, as it is not getting the vital nutrients it needs to survive. I have studied nutrition, food science, exercise physiology, and biology in my spare time, a bit in college, and during my short graduate school stint. I did know what can happen, so it was time for me to get back my life.

I have tried every diet in the book. No carbs, low carbs, no fruit, candy-all-day, and only-eat-yogurt-and-protein-shakes-all-day diets. Oh, and then there's the "don't eat after 6:00 p.m." rule, or the "fast before exercising rule" or my favorite—the Master Cleanse. All those diets just wore me out. I wasn't listening to my body and, quite frankly, my organs were working on overdrive to keep up with all the nonsense. Let me say this now: diets do not work! Sure, they work temporarily, and yeah, you'll hear, "Wow, you look amazing. What did you do? Tell me, tell me!" But when you head to Christmas dinner, then New Year's Eve, then Super Bowl Sunday, then out comes the Easter candy, summer cookouts, Fourth of July, birthday parties, Halloween candy hits the shelves next, festivals, Turkey Day, and now we are back at Christmas again . . . what are you gonna do then? Turn the other cheek? Let me say this: life is too damn short! Eat the cookie. Don't eat ten! They'll be there tomorrow! Don't tell me, "No, I'm starting my diet on Monday. I'm gonna eat all the cookies now and then I won't want them!" Nope. Not gonna happen. If you play that game, you will lose every time. Did the third cookie taste better than the first? Nooooo. How about the ninth? At that point, you ain't eating for the taste! You are bingeing! You are eating for the busyness, out of boredom, for the last-ditch effort, etc. Now that I eat slowly and control my portions, food tastes so much better! Gosh—food is amazing. It indulges all your sense at once.

So, based on those examples, let me reiterate: food is *not* your problem. We know that from the first few chapters. Food is not the enemy. Poor diet and lack of exercise have *nothing* to do with your excess weight. Lack of food has nothing to do with your gaunt anorexic body. The cause of your excess weight or lack thereof is in your mind (chapter 1). That's right. Last night's bingefest of pizza, nachos, and ice cream has nothing to do with your excess weight.

Train the Mind

Unprocessed emotions, such as mine, after the death of my mother, express themselves through undereating. This lack of nourishing my body was to block the pain I was experiencing from the loss of maternal love. Some people take drugs, overeat, abuse alcohol, abuse others. It's a choice to suppress, numb, or ignore the uncomfortable emotions one is experiencing.

I could give you a one-size-fits-all diet plan. I used to scour fitness magazines, searching for what the fitness model ate for Meal 1, Meal 2, Meal 3, etc. I would eat exactly what she ate, to the T. It didn't help that most of the time she was five nine and 140 pounds, with a medium build. I didn't have any of those measurements. The truth is that we are all unique, with different metabolisms, genetics, goals, and body types. Do not fall into the trap of reading that advertising! Relinquish the need to count calories, track points, skip meals, starve yourself with liquid meals because of the great myth of this country's marketing and obsessions with weight! You are special and unique, and if you take time to listen to your body and its internal tracking system, it will tell you what you need.

Listen to Your Body's Internal Hunger Cues

For those of you who have been pregnant, you know what listening to your body means. Remember that late-night snack you sent your honey out to get? Ice cream? Pickles? That was your body talking to you. A craving for pickles and ice cream simply means that the woman's body is in search of specific nutrients. Many midwives, doctors, and nurses believe that pregnancy cravings indicate a vitamin or mineral deficiency, and that the body is trying to make up for such deficiencies by making the foods with the needed nutrition seem particularly appealing. Bam! Your body is talking! Ever get that two o'clock slump? What's that, you ask? Did you eat a heavy lunch with grease and gluten and a soda? Any water since the moment you woke up? No? Only coffee, you say? Your body is spent from all the caffeine, heavy digesting, and lack of water. For the men out there, who haven't experienced pregnancy, ever gotten a cold? Did you want to thrown down a few slices of pizza and a pint of beer at the time? No way! Most likely, your were slowly munching on bland foods, warm liquids and foods, and giving your body a much-deserved digestive break.

Trust yourself. Eat when you are hungry, and stop when you are full. Tune into your body's wisdom about what you need. If you are choosing a fat-free diet or a sugar-free diet, you may be ingesting chemicals and other junk that could throw your whole body out of balance. This will definitely send your body into a trap of not knowing what it needs!

There are seven billion people on the planet, so there should be seven billion different diets! This also means there are seven billion different bodies. You are meant to look like yourself. Looking like you is a wonderful thing! Just because this person eats the Paleo way and that person is a vegan doesn't mean that either of those is the correct diet for you. Diets do not work. They do not stop the internal dialogue that is contributing to your weight. When you diet, you are unconsciously telling yourself that you are not enough.

Your weight, activity level, and/or health issues should be considered when you are thinking about what foods to eat. Listen to your body. It really does have a mind of its own . . . let it speak to you, and listen to it with wide-open ears.

Wide-Awake Eating

A way to free yourself from the chains of an eating disorder that consists of body hate, yo-yo dieting, and a gain weight–lose weight cycle, and to achieve a more balanced way of eating is to let your body guide you. Tune in to what it needs. Ignore the sponsored ads on the left side of your Facebook page hailing the next new diet, the pop ads on any website, spam e-mails, etc. Stop watching the news and reading the latest celebrity diet. You are done with all that. Say with me, "I. Am. Done!" Good. Feel better?

Start changing your relationship with food today. I promise: you will be healthier and happier if you let go of all the rules and diet trends.

1. *Track your emotional eating.* I know you all know how to stalk that ex-boyfriend/girlfriend's page on Facebook, so become your *own* investigator. What are you hiding in your own life? I want you to journal for the next three days what you eat, when you eat, and your emotions before, during, and after. If you didn't eat at certain mealtimes, why? What were you feeling? Your chart should look something like this:

   Time:
   Foods eaten:

Emotions before the meal:
Emotions after the meal:
I will give you some examples of what your chart might look like.
Time: 8:00 a.m.
Foods eaten: Sprouted grain toast with almond butter and bananas
Emotions before meal: Anxious
Emotions after meal: Full, satisfied, slightly nervous

The emotions are important here because much of the time we eat mindlessly, not focusing on chewing, not being grateful for the good offered to us this day, and shoving food into our mouths without even paying attention to portion or taste, smell, texture, etc.

Close your eyes, take small bites, and slow down. If you are feeling any negative emotions such as stress or anxiety, put the fork down and sit for a bit. Let the food make its way to the stomach. Take a few deep breaths and resume eating if the thoughts soften. If they don't, you may want to save the meal for later and do something soothing to ease your mind. Take a walk, read an uplifting quote, note, or book. Call a friend.

I have a great story about wide-awake eating. A few years ago, my family and I took a trip to Hershey Park (yes, an amusement park dedicated to all things chocolate in Pennsylvania.) We were attending a class called Chocolate University. They put four small pieces of chocolate in front of us. We were told to let each piece (one dark chocolate, one extra dark, one milk chocolate, and one with almonds) melt in our mouths without chewing it, move it around with our tongues, and savor the texture, taste, smell, etc. I gotta say I was worried for my hubby, who loves food and can eat a bag of M&Ms in two minutes flat. The chocolate tasted amazing, and it was so wonderful to savor it and really enjoy its flavor. I was much more satisfied with these small pieces of chocolate. My husband was too. Practice mindful eating. Sit down when you eat. Take it all in. If you are rushing, you won't be satisfied and may overeat. Eat when hungry. Use food as fuel.

2. *Do not count calories!* Throw calorie counting out the window. Do you think our ancestors had food labels? Do you think they cared how many calories they were eating? Eat what you want in moderation.

Let's use common sense here. You are thinking of eating a donut for breakfast which is about 200 calories. Instead, you should have something like a cup of Greek yogurt, one tablespoon of flax seeds, half a cup of blueberries and a dash of cinnamon, which has the same number of calories. Which meal will be healthier, satisfy your hunger and sweet tooth, and keep that metabolism humming? Which is the healthier option? Eat meals that contain quality calories like salads, beans, rice, lean proteins, many fruits and vegetables, nuts, and seeds. The processed foods (anything in a box or a bag in the grocery store or that even has a food label) need to go. All of it! Oreos, Cheezits, Doritos, etc. Do not keep them in your home. I know it is not a reality to eliminate them from your life completely, but take mindful, empowered steps to eat clean. Clean means whole, rich foods with no artificial this, preserved that. A wide-awake way of eating consists of healthy, whole foods that don't come with a food label at all. They are our earth's gifts, rich in vitamins, minerals, antioxidants, and natural yumminess to fuel our bodies.

3. *Do not label foods as good or bad.*

There is nothing either good or bad, but thinking makes it so!
–William Shakespeare

Cravings usually stem from this type of thinking. If there are no extremes, you can have whatever foods you want, whenever you want, instead of calling a food off-limits or bad. In this case, you don't eat or overeat certain things, because you can have them at any time! Then, instead of "cheating," you are indulging. Cheating is typically an all-you-can-eat binge on those "off-limits foods," which then results in the "I will start Monday" type of thinking. In the heat of anorexia, I thought fruit was bad, as well as corn and any type of fat—whether it be avocados, olive oil, butter, or the fat in a bag of pretzels. If it was fat-free, I was all over it! I excluded food groups as time went on, only eating protein (egg whites, hot dogs, salmon, chicken, etc.) That was not fun! I was chronically dehydrated, had the worst breath, and I was exhausted all the time! I was also *really* moody! And PMS had nothing to do with it. My poor body was void of the vitamins and minerals it needed to function at a healthy level. Do not be afraid of fat. Do not be afraid of carbs. Do not fear food. Do not be afraid of all natural fruit sugars. Yes, trans fat, added sugars, artificial sweeteners (Sweet'N Low, Truvia, Nutrasweet, etc.; again, mostly found in packaged foods and used in some restaurants) are awful, but if you stick with whole foods, you will never come across them. Ditch the convenient frozen dinners, boxed or packaged foods, please; you are eating chemicals! Would you pour a glass of laundry detergent as your beverage? Would you eat carpet deodorizer? Nope, so close your mouth to those foods whose ingredients you cannot pronounce.

4. *Eat real food.* Michael Pollan, a prolific author and pioneer of the organic movement, suggests three simple rules: "Eat food. Not too much. Mostly plants." Now I'm not suggesting that you go all-out vegan or ditch your favorite candy bar for good. I am suggesting you ditch "light" this or "diet" that. I was the queen of diet soda. I loved my lite and fat-free yogurt. I devoured the WOW chips and then sat on the toilet hours later. What fun is that? What kind of life do you want? I bet you would say one filled with energy; clear skin; a healthy digestive system; flexible limbs; and lean, strong muscles and bones. Eating chemicals will get you none of that. Believe me, I know! Eat lots of whole, organic foods. Your body will thank you.

5. *Go to a nutritionist.* Please go talk to a registered dietician, holistic nutritionist, or a primary care doctor who listens to your needs. Did you know that medical doctors receive very little to no nutrition training in medical school? They are taught mostly how to treat a disease through pharmaceuticals and surgery. Preventative medicine is something that is on the rise in this country, but so is the use of drugs to treat various symptoms of disease. There are many theories out there about how disease starts with the mind and the emotions. Anorexia most certainly starts with the mind. I stand by these theories and will speak more about them in the chakra-balancing chapter (chapter 8).

6. *Bash the scale!* Seriously, how is that number serving you, anyway? As part of my eating disorder therapy, I had to throw my scale in my driveway, shatter it against the ground, throw things at it, kick it, yell at it, etc. Let me tell you how cathartic that was! The media, the beauty magazines, TV—they are all trying to sell you something. More important, they are in the business of lowering your self-esteem, making you doubt your intuition, and then taking the money out of your wallet. There you are at the checkout counter buying another wrinkle cream and trying the latest weight-loss/pill/meal plan/book to get to that magic number on the scale. So what then? When you get to that magic number, what are you going to do then? In the midst of anorexia, there is no magic number. I thought there was, but there just wasn't. My self-esteem was so low at the time that no number would be magical or life-changing. I simply felt not good enough, so what the hell was a number gonna do? My mind was playing major tricks on me. I mean it. Throw a scale-bashing party! It will change your life.

7. *Make your own meals.* If you are cooking your own meals, you know *exactly* what is going into your food. Many restaurants mean well by providing healthier options, but the truth is, they are usually very salty, overbuttered, and portions that are meant for one person could feed two people or sometimes even three! The Internet is full of recipe databases that you can search at the drop of a hat. If you work two jobs or overtime, please get yourself a Crockpot and/or a slow cooker. Trust me, a recipe usually has five ingredients or so. Throw them in, set your timer, and it will be done when you get home from work.

8. *Focus on your greatest features.* Obsessing about cellulite or areas/body parts that you feel are "less than," or engaging in fat talk as you look at your body, are very self-destructive. There is nothing "wrong" with you! Play up your lovely shoulders and/or your strong calves. Wear a gorgeous necklace to showcase your neckline. Wear things that feel good to your body. Avoid tight-fitting clothing, as it can be uncomfortable and constrictive. When you are getting dressed in the morning, speak loving thoughts to your body. Look in the mirror and really own your beauty.

9. *Ideal body weight.* Was there a time in your life when you felt energetic, strong, and healthy? During that time you were most likely at your ideal body weight. It may not be the mythological weight that has been portrayed in the media or your anorexic weight. Avoid comparing your body to a friend's or to a popular celebrity. Every body is different, and we have different genetic and cultural traits. Bone structure and the size and shape of our bodies are different for everyone. If you are focused on eating a balanced, nutrient-rich diet, your body will follow your lead and maintain its ideal weight. Fuel it with a variety of foods, and give it proper rest by getting at least eight hours of well-deserved rest a night.

Your body was designed to know what it needs. Feed it rich, whole, healthy foods. The body doesn't know what to do with the processed stuff. Our elimination system has to work extra hard to rid the body of those toxins. Please be good to your body. Your body loves you. Love it back by nourishing it well. Remember, your body is only a vessel to express your beautiful soul. Nothing else.

Wide-Awake Reflection

Write a letter to your body and all its parts—even the parts you dislike—thanking them for all they do for you every day. I have always had a love-hate relationship with my hips, rear, and thighs. I have learned to love these parts because they brought life into the world. Our body is the temple that houses our beautiful soul. Let the image of the "ideal" thin body go. Celebrate what your body does for you!

> Dear Body,
> Thank you for all you have done for me. Thank you for my legs and feet, which allow me to walk and move in my home, the grocery store, the woods, and the malls, and on vacations, joyful family occasions, and girls' nights. Thank you for my arms and hands, which allow be to hug and to be hugged, to eat, brush my teeth, wash my face, and to type this book. Thank you for my mouth, lips, and tongue, which allow me to taste rich foods,

kiss, speak love and truth, and to nourish my cells every day with nutritious food and drink. Thank you for my eyes, which allow me to see God's kingdom of wondrous nature, as well as my family, friends, and children every day. Thank you for my nose and ears, which allow me to hear loving words, beautiful music, and smell God's creations. Thank you for my hips, rear, and thighs. These parts of my body are beautiful and are rich with womanly rights and wisdom. It is from there that I gave my birth to my two beautiful daughters, and I will love you and accept you now and forever.

You have never let me down. It is *I* that have let *you* down. I will cherish you and honor you, just as you have done for me. I will fill you with loving words, thoughts, and emotions, and healthy foods, and I will move you to keep you young and spry.

I love you,
Jensy

Your body is an absolute mirror of your mind. As you worry, your body shows it. As you love, your body shows it. As you are overwhelmed, your body shows it. As you are angry, your body shows it. Every cell of your body is being allowed or resisted by the way you feel. "My physical state is a direct reflection of how I feel," instead of "How I feel is a direct reflection of my physical state."

–Abraham Hicks

CHAPTER

5

Wide-Awake Body Movement

Exercise should be regarded as a tribute to the heart.
—Gene Tunney

When I first started out on my exercise journey, I was a calorie-burning machine. I used exercise as a tool to control my weight or to burn off more weight when I was dealing with anorexia. As a young child, I participated in many sports; I never excelled at just one but dipped my toes into several. It was fine because I stayed active, rode my bike, and played with my sisters and dog throughout my childhood. When things got busy in college, during the beginning stages of anorexia, the gym became my friend. I went to the gym to burn calories, plain and simple. I used the amount of time I could stay on a machine as a goal and then, unfortunately, the goal became how thin I could get. There is no fun in that. There is no healthy outcome from that sort of exercise. I continued on that journey for years, even as I recovered from anorexia. I would spend a lot of time at the gym lifting weights, doing sprints behind the gym, and pedaling for hours on the elliptical machine.

A few years ago, I started to take a kickboxing class in the group exercise room at the gym. I have never been one to learn choreography, and it took me awhile to pick it up, but I really enjoyed it. I felt alive when I was working out—something I had never experienced before. Sure, there were many highs with lifting weights, but this was way different. Having said that, I see many fitness competitors and bodybuilders thrive in this style of exercise. If that works for you and your mind, body, and soul are charged after your weight-lifting session, then please continue with your plan! For me, something was shifting. There was an energy, a goal, a spirit behind the movement. The music was loud and uplifting. I didn't care what my body looked like. The other gym-goers' energy was infectious! I was having fun, and I was exercising! As I took the class more and more, I began to feel tight in places I had never felt before. I knew yoga was calling my name to supplement this new lifestyle. I needed to stretch out those tight muscles.

I went to a yoga studio with one of my friends to take my first "real" class. I had done yoga in the past at gyms, by watching DVDs, etc., but never in an exclusive studio. The class was titled Yin Yoga. For all the nonyogis out there, this class is tough stuff. In yin yoga, poses are usually held for three to five minutes but can be held for as long as twenty minutes. Because of the long duration of the poses, it's important to practice patience—something I did not have a whole lot of at the time. For example, you are lying in a forward fold (seated position, legs spread, and head to floor, if possible) for a long time, stretching your muscle and getting deep into the connective tissue. It pulls, it stretches, and you must breathe deliberately! You can use props like pillows (bolsters), rolled up blankets, bands, etc., to help ease into the pose. When I left the class that evening, I felt like I had given my body the greatest gift. I felt refreshed and revitalized, and my body was given some love instead of the pounding and pushing to which I had subjected my muscles during the previous days. I was hooked on yoga!

That was three years ago, and haven't turned back. When I was exercising at the gym through my recovery, it was healthy. I was working my muscles and heart, but I just hadn't gotten a high. Runners know what I am talking about. Runner's high! Runner's high, as defined by Webster's is: a feeling of euphoria that is experienced by some individuals engaged in strenuous running and that is held to be associated with the release of endorphins by the brain. Euphoria? Who wouldn't want that?

I had found that with kickboxing, but even more so with yoga, my mind, body, and soul were fed in more ways than I could imagine.

I call this Your Wide-Awake Body Movement. Wide-Awake Movement, by my definition, is any physical activity that makes you feel alive, refreshed, and energized during the activity and at its conclusion. You should feel challenged without noticing the time. You will feel like you gave your body a gift of love and well-deserved attention. When you are doing this type of movement, your thinking is fun, exciting, and carefree. You aren't thinking about the calories you are burning or how much you hate this type of activity or how fat your thighs are. You move because it feels good. It's therapy, exercise, and meditation all rolled into one! How perfect is that?

I see many people slaving away at the gym, rowing strenuously or doing 500 crunches, and their bodies don't change and the looks on their faces seem grim. When I was anorexic, that was me. I was punished by this type of work and did not enjoy it. If you are struggling with the same phenomenon, you are probably not getting any results, and you feel unmotivated. Hence, you see the fall-off at the gym around February 15, following the New Year's Day blitz a month before. I was guilty of this. I am all gung ho when I start a new exercise regimen or diet plan and then fall off not seventy-two hours later. I simply was not feeding my soul with the type of physical activity I had chosen.

Make a commitment to yourself that you will devote thirty minutes to your Wide-Awake Movement every day. Stop engaging in the types of activities where you are only burning calories or are punishing yourself. Try to really feel how the body feels when you are exercising.

Exercise gives us energy and enables us to do the physical activities we enjoy. Your body craves this loving attention. It is a positive outlet for our energy and stress. It's so important to make healthy exercise part of your daily routine, and when you find a workout you enjoy, you're much more likely to do it.

What if I told you I could find an activity or exercise that you would enjoy every day or at least five days a week? That you will make it a priority every day because you can't wait to do it all over the next day? That you would feel even better than before you started the workout? Wouldn't that be "euphoric"? That you will never again despise exercising or use it as some form of self-punishment? Answer the following questions here to find a daily physical activity that soothes your soul . . .

Wide-Awake Body Movement Reflection

Get out your journal, and let's start brainstorming to find the types of physical activities that are most suited to you.

1. What was your favorite physical activity as a child? Did you enjoy running? Dancing? Hopscotch? Walking in the woods? Did you excel in any sport as a child? Whatever you answer is, go out and try a few of these activities! If you answered "walking in the woods," you might be a hiker or even a yogi. If you answered hopscotch, you might enjoy kickboxing or Zumba (Latin dancing exercise class). If you were a ballerina, try a barre class. Soccer, hockey, softball, tennis, and golf are all great sports to play as an adult. Play around with these activities, and let you body "run" with them!
2. Do you like working out with friends or are you a "more to yourself" kinda gal? Try any sort of group exercise class at the gym. Step classes, weight-training classes, and spinning are all great ways to socialize and get in a great, butt-kicking, fun workout! If you have children, run around the block with them, shoot hoops, or ride bikes. If you enjoy working out alone, there are plenty of wonderful DVDs on the market to pump you up. You can also take up running or power walking, or your throw your own dance party in your room!
3. Do you enjoy high-intensity, butt-kicking workouts or do you prefer low-impact, less strenuous, but nonetheless challenging workouts? What suits your body at this stage in your life? What types of injuries must you be mindful of? Check yourself before you wreck yourself by diving into a fitness program.
4. Are you competitive? If you are, check out CrossFit or military-style boot camps in your area. Also, join that adult league you love! I promise these workouts will feed your competitive nature. If you are not competitive, try yoga. The basis of yoga is not to compete with anyone else in the room. Each person is on his or her own individual yoga journey.

I wish I could give you a list of weight-lifting routines and a cardio plan to follow. I tried that in my brief stint as a personal trainer. That's not me, and it's simply not fair to give a one-size-fits-all approach to any of you. The above questionnaire will help you find your Wide-Awake Movement. After filling out the survey—did you find your "it"? Is it dancing? Is it being in nature, hiking? Is it surfing? Boxing?

Whatever it is, do it. Do it five or six days a week for at least thirty minutes. Your body needs to move. You owe it to your body to keep it strong, healthy, and active. Write it on your calendar now. Make that appointment to take care of you.

How to Start Your Wide-Awake Body Movement

Again, as I have learned, we are all different, and what works for one body may not work for another. I have seen stay-at-home moms get fit and happy by joining CrossFit, but I have also seen another stay-at-home mom with a similar build get fit and happy walking around my neighborhood five days a week for sixty minutes.

In the past year, I have stopped working out consistently. I think my mind, body, and spirit needed a break from a regular exercise regimen and just wanted to move when it felt like it. But now I'm ready, like some of you, to get back to a consistent Wide-Awake Exercise Routine. This is how I got back on track and how you can too!

1. *Start somewhere.* It doesn't matter how long, what type of movement, what intensity. Just do what you can do, today. Don't be so hard on yourself when you hit the pavement or the weights. We have all been a beginner at some point in our lives, so you are not alone. Do five minutes of physical activity. Do ten. Do something!
2. *Make appointments for your daily physical activity.* If you don't pencil it in or schedule it, it will most likely never happen. Life happens: kids get sick, it snows, you forget that you promised a date with your best friend, etc.
3. *Eat that frog at five a.m.* An old saying is that "If the first thing you do each morning is to eat a live frog, you can go through the day with the satisfaction of knowing that that is probably the worst

thing that is going to happen to you all day long!" Your "frog" is the one you are most likely to procrastinate on if you don't do something about it now! So my workouts are early, and then they are not hanging over my head all day.
4. *Track your progress*: there are so many applications on smart phones that do it for you. This keeps me motivated and helps me stay on track with healthy exercise.
5. *Reward yourself*: A new workout outfit, a brand-new seasonal top or a big pat on the back. You deserve rewards for sticking with it, acknowledging your self-worth and making your health a priority!

So I hope for you, that you have learned that the latest fitness craze to buzz through the media outlets may not be the perfect fit for you! Give yourself the gift of exploring how your body and mind feel when you engage in physical activity. Let's quit engaging in unhealthy exercise behaviors. Move because it feels good! Find out what works, start, and then make a commitment to yourself that you will keep with it as part of your healthy balance triad of mind, body, and spirit!

> Those who think they have not time for bodily exercise will sooner or later have to find time for illness.
> –Edward Stanley

III

Spirit

CHAPTER

6

Relationships

Relationships are assignments. They are part of a vast plan for our enlightenment—the Holy Spirit's blueprint by which each individual soul is led to greater awareness and expanded love. Relationships are the Holy Spirit's laboratories in which He brings together people who have the maximum opportunity for mutual growth. He appraises who can learn most from whom at any given time and then assigns them to each other. Like a giant computer, He knows exactly what combination of energies, in exactly what context, would do the most to further God's plan for salvation. No meetings are accidental.

–Marianne Williamson

You must love yourself before you love another. By accepting yourself and fully being what you are, your simple presence can make others happy. You yourself, as much as anybody in the entire universe, deserve your love and affection.

–Buddha

This two quotes were game changers for me, back when I first read them! Isn't it great to know that every awful relationship you ever had made you a better person? They were all here to enhance your life by either helping you grow, strengthening you, or complimenting your journey. Not all relationships are meant to last forever. A part of your life's journey is to have a relationship so difficult that it brought you to your knees, because it would make you grow into the person you were meant to be. Yes, that guy you dated in high school who broke up with you or the friend you lost over a disagreement can be the greatest asset to your life! I'm dead serious. Consider all your relationship as gifts! Be thankful for those experiences because they helped you learn and grow! These people came into your life just to strengthen you.

Relationships have not always been easy for me. As a young child, I had friendships that were fun, carefree, and silly, but I never experienced the depth of a true friendship until my mother died. The evening of the day she died, my dearest of friends came to my home to offer their support, love, and prayers. I had never known a love so deep and pure. Real friends rise to the occasion when you need them the most. When I got to college, we separated and grew in different directions but still kept in touch. Some of my high school friends are still my nearest and dearest friends. They have accepted me for who I am, despite all the changes. While I was in college I had some not-so-great boyfriends, and all the while I was still dating my high school soul mate. It was after my Wide Awakening that I realized that those men were just bumps on the road of life to help me learn more about my infinite inner and outer beauty. I hope that resonates with you—that some of your failed relationships are only bringing you to the right ones.

Are you currently in a bad relationship/friendship/family squabble that is dragging you down? I know we all think we are gonna live forever, but we are not. Our days are numbered. Life is short and has its aches and pains, but life is also beautiful. We have free will and it's ultimately you who decide with whom you will spend your time. Fear is what is holding you back from claiming your worth.

One of the most exciting principles, and one of the easiest to understand, that is helpful in deciding whom to spend your time and energy on, is the Pareto Principle introduced in 1906 by Italian economist Vilfredo Pareto. He observed that 80 percent of the land in Italy was owned by 20 percent of the population. This principle can be applied to so many things: the economy, your wardrobe, your diet, etc.

In essence, many of us are wasting 80 percent of our time on low-value relationships. Twenty percent of our friends account for 80 percent of our pleasure, enjoyment, and fun. This principle holds true with the mega social networking site Facebook. Twenty percent of your Facebook friends account for 80 percent of your pleasure, time, and energy.

Stop wasting your time and energy on people who give you constant drama, headaches, and negative energy! You are the average of the people with whom you spend the most time. So choose the good seeds!

So let's say you are engaging with ten people a day. They can be partners, kids, teachers, coworkers, bosses, parents, etc. About two of those people (maybe more, especially if you have two or more children) account for the happiness and well-being of your life. I'm not saying that you shouldn't talk to your boss, friend, etc., but don't spend your time worrying about the other eight. Give as much time and energy to the two relationships that do matter, and don't let the others take away from the two that matter.

Don't sweat the small stuff—or in this case, the small people—in your lives!

How many times have you gotten angry about the guy who cut you off in traffic? What about the customer service rep you spoke to on the phone who left you on hold? Or worse, the old boyfriend or drama queen friend whom you keep giving chances because you *know* they are going to change eventually? Those experiences can affect your mood, and guess who feels that? The two who matter.

I believe each one of us should put together a Wide-Awake Team. Your team consists of people who possess the following traits. I have used the acronym SELF:

- S is for Supportive
- E is for Encouraging
- L is for Loving
- F is for Forgiving

Disclaimer: before you go out seeking these people in your life, you must believe these things about yourself first. (Head back to chapter 3 if you need a refresher.) You must be supportive, encouraging, loving, and forgiving to yourself before you fully form your team and enter into a healthy, fulfilling relationship. If you are unsupportive of yourself, you will attract unsupportive people. That's a guarantee. Believe me, I know. Remember, I'm your guinea pig!

Now Presenting Your Wide-Awake Team

Zen Friends

A friendship between two individuals where there is a give and take, an ebb and flow, a wax and wane. There will be good times, sad times, and just okay times. In my thirties I have found Zen friends who are SELF, because I have become more supportive of my own needs and desires, encouraging myself to do better, try harder, love myself unconditionally, and forgive my own mistakes. Until you can fully develop these characteristics in yourself, you will not find Zen friends. The friends are Zen because they too have learned to be supportive, encouraging, loving, and forgiving of themselves. You can only reap what you sow.

No doubt there will be times in your friendship where one of you is not feeling so encouraging. That's when it's the other's turn to step into the ebb and flow of the relationship and lift her friend up.

A Zen friend calls you when you're sick, sees the best in you, is by your side in troubled times, and is someone with whom you can be yourself. You can be silly, goofy, and vulnerable with these friends.

Wide-Awake Soul Mates

Most of us have kissed a few frogs before we met our wide-awake soul mate. The reason for that is that we have to know what we *don't* want in a relationship so we can see what we *do* want.

Your relationship with your wide-awake soul mate must allow for the following:

- You must feel safe being yourself around him or her—the most authentic, vulnerable version of you.

- Your wide-awake soul mate supports your career endeavors and your hopes and dreams and goals; cares for your family, your friendships, and your life outside of the relationship.
- Your wide-awake soul mate expresses affection through physical touch, kind words and acts, and thoughtful gifts.
- You spend quiet quality time with one another with few or no distractions.
- Your wide-awake soul mate exemplifies the SELF qualities listed above.
- You and your wide-awake soul mate have shared interests, hobbies, and philosophies.

Before you begin to pursue any romantic relationship, you *must* review the self-love chapter. If you are looking for someone to be supportive, encouraging, loving, and forgiving, you *must*—I repeat, *must*—be working on developing these traits within yourself or you must possess them already. You cannot go looking for these traits in another person to fill your needs. You must find them within yourself *first*. Your happiness will *never* be found in another person. The relationship should complement you and your infinite goodness.

It took me a long time to realize this. I kept searching for someone to make me happy. Oh, my poor spouse! When I finally realized that I was solely responsible for my happiness, my relationships flourished, I removed from my life the toxic people bringing me down, and found the right people to enhance my journey.

Forgiving family

In meeting and talking with many men and women about their most challenging relationships, I have found that family relationships seem to be the most difficult. We are born into a family. The universe handpicked you to enter your family to help you grow into your best self. I know, I know—some of you don't want to hear that, but sometimes the truth hurts.

A forgiving family member values your opinion and supports your goals and dreams. This member listens to your woes and calms you down. They encourage you to live your best life.

We have lived with these people day in and day out for at least eighteen years of our lives. There are family patterns that have developed over time. Jealousy, communication challenges, divorce, disappointment, and death may have occurred at some point. If you are having a challenging time with one or more family members, you may want to avoid topics that bring discord, because, after all, they are your family.

If you have exhausted all communication efforts to achieve some accord, and you have forgiven, encouraged, supported, and loved your family member, it may be time to love that person from a distance. Your family will always be blood. There will always be love there. In order to heal and show yourself some self-respect, it may be time to take a step back.

I have seen this go one of two ways. The family member awakens, matures, and grows and realizes that you are responsible for your own life, and they are responsible for theirs. Much family discord arises from parents trying to control their children's decisions and actions. Your child will slip, will fall, will make mistakes. We all do. That's how we learn.

As a mother, I have found that if I love my children for who they are, not for who I want them to be, parenting becomes simpler.

The second scenario is when the family member shuts you out completely and never moves past forgiveness and acceptance. Don't pretend to be something you are not to get a person to like you. You are not living authentically, and this will set you up for an unfulfilling, unhappy life. It is simply the other person's issue, not yours.

Acceptance is key for you to heal this relationship. Focus on what is. Unconditional love and acceptance are the only worthwhile constants. If the family member cannot accept you for who you are, and you are accepting them for who they are, then it's time to pull back from the relationship and start living your life.

It will be painful and hard at first, but you must do this for you. Your happiness. You are not meant to live a life of crappiness. Take ownership of that. You will never change someone, and you must never change who you are to accommodate someone's expectations of you. Seek out the family members who are SELF, and surround yourself with their love and be strong.

You are solely responsible for your experience of life. You are not responsible for someone else's experience of their life. A real relationship can emerge when you stop taking on that responsibility. Be strong; do not back down. For the most part, after you have stayed strong for a while, you will start inspiring that person to do better. Be better. Just maybe, the person will come around. After all, it's Love that binds us all.

Helpful heroes

These team members are your priests, nurses, doctors, fitness instructors, teachers, inspirational leaders and healers, therapists, famous philosophers, and perhaps even a stranger on your journey.

As I travel through my life, I look back on all the helpful heroes who have crossed my path. There are millions of people in this world who want to help others. When my mom died, I had a football-team–size group of helpful heroes who wanted to ease my pain. As a brazen sixteen-year-old, I felt that I had the "grieving stuff" down. I had priests, therapists, maternal figures, and warrior teachers who cared deeply about helping me with my suffering. I was having none of it! My ego jumped right out in front and proclaimed, "I don't need your help, I can handle this on my own."

Look where that got me . . .

The truth is, we are all here to help one another. There is a story we tell ourselves that if we ask for help, we are imperfect. Don't let the fear of being judged by others stop you from asking for help. You must be willing to take that first small step in asking for help. It's the human connection that binds us all to help one another in need. It is truly why we are here.

If you keep reaching out for help, and you are not receiving it, you are asking the wrong person. That person is emotionally unavailable to you or may need help themselves, and you two are just not the perfect match at this time. It's no one's fault, really. It's the universe's way of helping you find the right hero for your life.

Reach out to the SELF people. Use that small, still, quiet voice inside you to seek out those helpful heroes. They are all around you. Sometimes it is the grocery clerk at your favorite supermarket who makes a thoughtful remark about your healthy food choices, or the quiet, shy mother in your child's carpool line who compliments you on your parenting, or your mother-in-law, who gives you great tips and recipes to improve your family dinners.

Life is an experience and a constant, steady stream of learning. Helpful heroes are some of the greatest educators during our lives. Take their golden nuggets of wisdom, hold them in your heart, and let them carry you through your brightest and darkest days.

You have now successfully identified your wide-awake team members. Be grateful for these people, because they truly love and care for you.

The following are the types of team members you want to avoid.

Poisonous pals

These people blame others and/or events for their problems or failures. They take no responsibility for their circumstances. They blame the economy, their parents, their in-laws, teachers, their past, etc. Poisonous pals:

- are ungrateful, uninspired, and unexcited; they constantly spew complaints;
- focus on the problems, not the solutions;
- take from the relationship but rarely give;
- make you feel that the friendship is one-sided and that you are constantly being supportive, encouraging, loving, forgiving without getting the same in return. The reason for this is that they aren't feeling that way about themselves. These pals are trying to get that from you, and it's never going to happen.

We all go through pain. It is certain that we will lose a loved one, and that we will experience hard times. Yes, it's important to be there for a friend, but there may come a point in a friendship where you feel like you are a constant source of consolation and help and that you listen to a never-ending stream of complaints. You are not the other person's therapist. You are that person's friend. You cannot solve your friends' problems. It will drag you down if you are not careful. When you are starting to notice that you are constantly giving of yourself and really feel no friendship from the other side, then it's time to have a talk with your poisonous pal about what you are feeling. If all goes well, you may be able to rekindle your friendship. This may be just the lesson your poisonous pal needs. If your "friend" takes it personally and is not willing to see your side, you must love yourself enough to let go of the toxicity and move on to find Zen friends who will enhance your life. Remember, you are not responsible for anyone's happiness but your own.

Everyone in your life is helping you on your journey to experience life to its fullest. You have free will to decide whether each relationship is one you wish to continue. If you cannot escape the relationship (with your parents or siblings, for example), the person is your teacher. Yes, the individual will push your buttons, but he or she is here to teach you patience, unconditional love, and compassion.

If you are drawn to poisonous pals, you are still learning the lesson on how to love yourself fully and openly. This is part of your journey, and it's okay; you will get through it and be even stronger for it on the other side. Surround yourself with friends who exhibit SELF characteristics. Even in times when you are not feeling SELF, seek out Zen friends. But misery does love company, so be mindful with whom you spend your time.

Loser life partners

By my definition, loser life partners can be described in the following way. They:

- are immature;
- throw temper tantrums;
- get jealous very easily. (Don't be flattered by jealousy . . . they are immature, insecure, and controlling. If they are not letting you live your own life, let them go! Fast.);
- bring up the past;
- chip away at your self-esteem by calling you names, insulting your family members, and putting down your friends, hobbies, interests, and job;
- blame everyone and everything else for their problems;
- are very dramatic and exciting because they pump you up, but then they drag you down!
- take from the relationship but rarely give.

A loser life partner is not a "loser." There are no losers in the world. This is just a losing relationship for you. You are on different paths in your journey. In a healthy relationship, you are in two separate cars driving on the same path, maybe at slightly different points, but on average, side by side. A loser life partner is similar to a poisonous pal except for the romantic element and the daily flirting and affection that goes on in a day-to-day relationship. It's a much deeper, more time-invested commitment and is therefore a harder relationship to let go.

We've all had 'em! At least one. If you haven't had one, consider yourself very lucky. I am here to tell you that those all-night crying sessions adorned with empty ice cream cartons and empty Kleenex boxes are history, baby.

If you have exhausted all your resources, such as daily talks, breaking up and making up, and marriage counseling; you are having more bad days than good days; and—even worse—you are on the receiving end of mental or even physical abuse, get out now! Do not turn back. Get out of there and figure out the rest once you have left. I know there is at least one person who can help you get back on your feet again.

Difficult partners present themselves to awaken us to the deeper lessons that we are now ready to learn.

If you are currently in a romantic situation with a loser life partner, do your best to leave or work to improve the relationship drastically. Reach down deep within yourself, reflect on what's not working, and tell yourself that you deserve better than what you are getting from the relationship. You must take action. You can pack your bags or head to therapy. The relationship needs help and work.

If you decide to break up, it's okay to be alone, no matter what some relationship book says or a magazine promotes. Being with the wrong person can be lonelier than being alone. You will find that once the initial mourning for the relationship is over, you will feel more confident, free, and laser-focused on the things that you do want from a relationship. You will definitely know what you don't want from a relationship, so take that with you on the rest of your journey. That's the silver lining. Adios!

Throughout my life, I have had very few breakups. I am married to my first boyfriend. I still keep in touch with all my high school friends. I have never cut off ties with any family member. I feel very blessed. It wasn't until my awakening that I experienced some failed relationships.

After my awakening, I embraced all of me and stopped living behind a mask. I started living *my* truth and needed no one's approval. I got criticism at the time from one person.

You have enemies? Good. That means you've stood up for something, sometime in your life.
—Winston Churchill

I had a friend once who started blaming me for things I said and did and who created drama and started arguments with me. I began to doubt the new anorexic, free, happy me. I was ready to back down about who I am, what I wanted to do with my life, and the success I was having. I was willing to throw it all away so she would stop criticizing me, and I could stop hurting her, until I realized this one thing.

Hurt people hurt people. Yep, that quote is back again!

Who was I really hurting if I backed down about who I truly am? Me!

She wasn't battling me. She was battling herself. My truth was triggering her. When you truly accept yourself for all that you are, good and bad, and you are living authentically and, for the most part, happily, that can trigger someone in your life. They are missing the "old" you. You were the one not taking action, the one agreeing to everything the person said, the one who was accommodating to the other person's needs all the time. When you finally decide that you are not responsible for making someone else happy all the time, some "stuff" can sometimes hit the big ol' fan!

After a period during which I did not conform to her pressure, she let her grudges go and started becoming inspired by my daily actions, and our relationship grew again and became stronger. This story had a happy ending.

Some stories do not.

I had another friend who wanted me to be more like her. In a way, she was "peer-pressuring" me to be more like her. I was engaging in behaviors I did not feel right in doing.

I was not having any of that! My awakening gave me the confidence to know I did not want that kind of friend in my life. To this day, we do not speak. I feel no anger, bitterness, resentment, or guilt about having let the friendship go. The friendship was not right for either of us. It was just a stepping-stone and a learning experience for both of us. If I saw her somewhere, I would give her a great big hug and wish her only the very best. We both deserve that.

I believe strongly that we were only meant to know each other for a season, not a lifetime.

"People come into your life for a reason, a season, or a lifetime. When you know which one it is, you will know what to do for that person."

I give you these two examples because I want you to see that you can walk away from a toxic relationship. Neither of you has done anything wrong. You were just at different points on your journey. It takes two to make a relationship work, but it takes courage for one to let go.

Wide-Awake Reflection

Grab your journal and make four columns. List your Zen friends, wide-awake soul mate, helpful heroes, and forgiving family members. This is your wide-awake team, and you are the leader. Are any of the columns blank? For the next twenty-eight days, I want you actively to seek SELF teammates. Is there a relationship that you have not been fostering? Maybe it's your priest at church whom you are too shy to approach. Have a word with him after church. Tell him you enjoyed his sermon. Reach out to your mail carrier. He does a good job getting your mail to you, right? Make him or her some baked goods, extend a friendly hello, and strike up a conversation. Make a commitment to spend time with your team. Schedule it on your calendar. These relationships are what enrich your life.

On the next page, list your poisonous pals, loser life partners, and maybe some less forgiving family members. Make a challenge for the next twenty-eight days to assess the relationships here. Observe as a fly on the wall the time that you spend with them. Are these relationships healthy and safe in your life? Are they worth salvaging? Don't let fear stop you from leaving the situation. In the column below their names, list the pros and cons of each relationship. My dad always says, "If the good things outweigh the bad things, then the relationship is worth saving." I like that advice.

Good luck!

CHAPTER

Exploring Your Spirituality

Religion is for people who are scared to go to hell. Spirituality is for people who have already been there.

–Bonnie Raitt

Anorexics and people struggling with their weight are aware that they have been to hell. It's a very lonely, dark place to live. Spirituality can help to connect the inner you and heal your soul, which wants so badly to be loved. Many fail to connect with that inner guide because we are so busy with the emotional baggage, the constant negative thoughts about ourselves, and the plain busyness of life.

Every morning, when my alarm goes off at 6:00 a.m., I hit "Snooze" a few times, jump out of bed, brush my teeth, splash water on my face, and get the kids ready and out the door by 7:20. When they leave, I plop down in my chair and have some "me" time. That was just an eighty-minute sprint! In my glorious, pink chaise lounge chair, I read spiritual passages, spiritual blogs, take deep breaths, and do a short meditation.

Flashback to my twenties. I wasn't taking any time-outs or little refreshers like that throughout the day. I was driving to work without eating breakfast, sitting in traffic for almost two hours, weaving in and out of lanes, picking up a diet soda and bagel before sitting down at my desk, and cranking out an eight-to-ten-hour workday. Then off to happy hour, make dinner, and pass out in front of the TV exhausted. Then I would do it all over again the next day. You can see why the bottom dropped out for me, and I relapsed into depression. I wasn't feeding my spirit. I was completely burned out! I was a busy little bee, buzzing around town and not giving my soul any attention! Not even five minutes!

For the last twenty years or so, I was the biggest skeptic about faith, spirituality, a higher power, God, Buddha—whatever you call your Source.

I was in a dark, lonely place for so long, as you know, that I chose the "everything bad happens to me" attitude and chose to live there. I blamed everything and everyone for my problems. (Please don't ever do that! It takes you straight to Nowhereville!) I didn't believe that everything happens for a reason. I just believed that I was meant to live a scorned life, and I would stay in a place of suffering with anorexia all my life.

When my daughters were born, that all vanished. I saw the hope, love, and dreams for them waiting to be fulfilled. Now, I don't encourage you to have children to find your faith and spirituality, but that's what it took for me to find the Way. You may be in the middle of a breakup or your parents' divorce, have lost your job, or you could just be exploring your purpose. You don't have to be down and out to want answers to important questions like, "Why does your Source cause bad things to happen in your life?"

I couldn't believe I was so lucky to have been given the two precious gifts of life and inspiration. It made me wonder why, since I had been so depressed and had suffered with anorexia for so long. I knew I had to step up, grow up, and explore why I had received this second lease on life.

That's where my faith came in. Some higher power had given me a second chance in life. You hear about second chances all the time. People who have near-death experiences, emotional breakdowns, car accidents, death sentences, repeated hospital visits, tragedies, injuries, etc., and who come back with more strength, more gratitude, and less gloom and doom. They overcome the odds to live harder, braver, and better for having done so.

The births of my daughters led me to believe in something more—something so grand, and so full of Love. There just had to be a higher power.

My yoga practice centered me in that space. Physical blocks were removed, and I was able to receive more as result. At the end of every yoga practice, after you have completed your series of *asanas* (poses or postures), you enter into *savasana*. *Savasana* is a five-to-ten-minute—and in some classes, longer—meditation where you let it all go. Your physical body melts into the floor in a prone position. You let your legs fall to the side, and your palms face upward to receive the light and love.

Many people get uncomfortable in this space because their mind races. Mine still does, depending upon the amount of stress I am feeling that day. "I have to go grocery shopping, I smell, I'm sweaty, I feel bad I said no to that invitation by my friend for coffee." This is your monkey mind doing its dance. It will do its thing, but it's your job to be aware of the thoughts and breathe into them. Don't judge them; stay neutral.

After practicing yoga for a few years, I wanted to deepen my meditation practice. I had just seen *Eat, Pray, Love*, a movie starring Julia Roberts, based on a true story about the author, Elizabeth Gilbert's journey of self-discovery. She eats her way through Italy (how fun!), meditates and prays her way through India, finds inner peace, and then, ultimately, finds the love of her life after extensive soul-searching in Bali.

I had my moment in the mountains of Virginia on one of my personal retreats. This time I was ready to take it a step further in an ashram for a weekend stay. I stayed in my home state of Virginia. Maybe one of these days I will set out on a journey like Elizabeth Gilbert.

Yogaville, a spiritual yoga resort/center, is set in the heart of Virginia, in the middle of nowhere, in a picturesque setting of mountains, valleys, and quiet wonder. A perfect oasis for reflection, serenity, and de-stressing. It is located far away from human habitation, and there are no stores, gas stations, or highways nearby. The ashram is a place to practice stillness, meditation, and yoga, and to let the mind and body rest, so the spirit can hear its own voice. I was headed on a spiritual vacation.

I pulled into the ashram, excited to be taking part in this amazing weekend. The weekend was more than I could possibly have imagined. I learned so much while I was there.

I was apprehensive when I entered the meditation center for the first time. I had done some meditating in the past but mostly through prayers, long walks, yoga class, and hikes. I managed to get myself into a state that was peaceful and still, but I did need a lot more work. No drugs, alcohol, or caffeine are allowed at the retreat. The rooms do not have televisions or radios. Your cell phone barely gets reception. Some meals are to be eaten in silence. I enjoyed learning that I rush through meals and barely chew. I found that when I ate in silence, I was more attuned to my senses, savoring each bite, eating more slowly, and not overeating. Hence, the discovery of wide-awake eating (chapter 4). Before I went to bed, I would journal about my day, relax my mind and body, and my sleep was more peaceful. When I would pass the staff members and other resort guests, the silence allowed me to look into their eyes and see their beautiful souls, which helped me realize that we are all seeking the same thing.

Everybody seems to be looking for peace there. We all have had our share of struggles, and that won't end. Life is a series of ups and downs. We may lose an important person(s) in our life, or a job, a friend, or a pet; suffer from an illness; feel depressed, lonely and/or sad. It is important to process these hard times through grieving, journaling, talking it out, and then seeing the beauty of the lesson and marching on because you are stronger for it. Sometimes, in this busy world we live in, we don't get a chance to listen to our feelings. We keep pushing and doing and forget to give our soul the love and attention it needs. Many visitors at the ashram had been drug addicts and alcoholics. After spending time at the ashram, they were able to find the inner peace they were searching for. Addictions are healed, and hearts are mended there. Many started working there and ultimately became yoga teachers and spiritual leaders. During my stay, I processed some heavy emotions that were lying on the surface. I opened my heart and mind to the idea of finally letting them go. The peace that comes from surrendering is pure freedom.

During my stay, I ate very healthfully. The ashram's kitchen only serves fresh, organic vegetarian meals. No chicken or turkey! I was apprehensive about this, thinking, *I need my protein!* What I found is that vegetarianism is not that bad, and the protein thing is a myth. Again, I was open and willing to try what they had to offer. The meals were delicious and filling. Food served as fuel and clean nutrition, and I felt great. Six months later I decided to adopt the vegetarian lifestyle and haven't turned back since.

On the second night at the ashram, I experienced the migraine of my life! Yes, a big, fat, throbbing migraine. In Lise Bourbeau's book *Your*

Body Is Telling You: Love Yourself, she points out, "Migraines are directly linked with the I AM. They are most common in those who will not allow themselves to live according to their true nature. If a teenager, for example, dreams of being an artist, but allows himself to be influenced by his parents into another line of work, he can suffer from migraines as long as he does not allow himself to be what he wants TO BE." I was releasing all the years of not experiencing my true self. I wrote down all my goals as far as what I wanted my life to be, without any judgments and outside influences. I went to bed early that evening and woke up with a clear mind and a heart open to the life I had always been waiting for. The pain I felt that night is something I cannot describe, but I can't tell you how worth it, it was.

After I left that Sunday, I made a decision that meditation was always going to be a part of my life. It helped with the anorexic thoughts that still sometimes enter my mind. So I started with basic meditation 101. I want to show you what I did.

Meditation 101

I think most of us have an idea that meditation means sitting cross-legged and repeating a mantra (ommmm) or concentrating on a noise for a time until the mind is free from all thoughts, maybe while wearing a turban or all-white clothes. That's some mystified image the media has put out or something you see in spiritual or religious textbooks.

The truth is, there is no right or wrong way to meditate. You make it what you want it to be. In fact, there are many different, easy ways to do it. Meditation means to reflect, contemplate, or think. That's it, and that's all. You need to find what works for you and what you are most comfortable doing.

There are many ways to meditate other than just sitting in a traditional meditation pose. Some go for a long run, journal their thoughts, go on long car rides, walk the beach, spend time in nature, etc. It's a time away from life's dramas and busyness to get centered, refocus, and reflect. It's a time to connect with your true self—full of gratitude, love, and dreams.

Meditation is a little spiritual gift you give to yourself and others. Looking back on my life, I was always doing, going, and busying myself to distract from who I really was. Whether I was on a long run, in my car, or sitting still, I was thinking about my faults and mistakes and beating myself up with negative thoughts and feelings like, "You are fat, you are stupid, why did I say that? etc." Now, when those feelings come up during times of reflection, I choose a healthier, gentler thought reflecting self-forgiveness, gratitude, self-compassion, and kindness. Instead of trying to be so perfect, I take the thoughts as they are and choose a better one. It doesn't happen every time, but we can only expect progress—not perfection—from ourselves.

The miracle of meditation is no secret. The most recent research suggests that meditation can reduce stress and alleviate anxiety and depression. When I first tried meditation at the eating disorder treatment center, I was forcing the issue. I desperately wanted to stop being depressed, so I was hasty with the traditional practice of focusing on the breath. As I stuck with it (even on days I did not feel like it), it got easier.

Although I feel that you can meditate through exercise, writing, and long baths, I also know that there may not be an opportunity for those things. It's just like learning basic math. Yes, calculators have been invented, but there may be some cases where they are simply not convenient. So I believe it's important to know the basics of meditation, just as we need to know the basics of math.

Introduction to Meditation

1. Get seated in a comfortable position with your spine upright and your chest lifted. It is extremely important to have your back straight so your breath can flow freely. You will need to sit on two folded blankets, a pillow, or something to lift your hips at least two to four inches higher than your knees. This is done to protect your lower back, as you will be seated here for a significant period of time and will want to be as physically comfortable as possible.
2. Set your intention. At the beginning of every yoga class, your teacher usually asks you to set an intention. An intention can be a prayer, an affirmation, or a goal you have for the day. It helps you stay in touch with your core values and how you want to live your life that day. You could say something like, "I will do the best I can today. I will show kindness to myself and others today."

3. Begin breathing with awareness. Inhale softly as you bring attention to any aches, pains, or tension in any parts of your body. Breathe into those parts. Exhale by letting go, softening, and releasing into those areas. Scan the body. As your body relaxes, your mind will, too. Let your breath settle into a rhythmic pattern.
4. If your mind wanders to your day or a heavy thought, bring it back gently to the breath. Notice that you may be anxious, tense, or maybe relaxed. Invite your mind to relax. Just breathe in and out. You may even use a mantra here, like, "I am safe, all is well, I am doing great," and then continue to breathe. I find if use an "I am" affirmation, it eases the tension and the stressful thoughts.
5. Focus on soothing images as your eyes stayed closed. Keep breathing gently and softly.

Many people set timers when meditating. I find that to be helpful, as I know you have given yourself at the minimum five minutes of your day to get quiet and restore your mind, body, and spirit to the state your true self lives in the moments free of life's responsibilities/chatter/dramas.

Commit to seven days in a row of this practice, at the least. Then make it a daily part of your routine.

Meditation has shown to relax the mind and keep you focused on your intention for your life. It can cultivate your intuition, where your inner peace lies. If you stay with this practice, it is likely that more positive things will happen in your life. I know that this will enhance your recovery as it has mine.

Intuition

Intuition, as defined by *Merriam Webster's*, means "quick and ready insight." It is the core of who we really are. We came into the world as light at the moment the sperm hit the egg. At the core of our being is love. Your intuition can sometimes be called your higher self, inner healer, your soul, your spirit, your wise mind. Your intuition knows exactly who you are and how to live a happy, healthy life. It knows no fear or lack thereof. You are because you live.

You must be tapped into your intuition to be balanced in your life. If you are not, things can get out of balance and you can become disconnected from your authentic self. You begin to doubt your inner guide and go down the wrong path. You second-guess all your decisions and rely on others to make the decisions for you. Anorexia definitely distracts from knowing the real you.

As a kid, I remember seeing Fred Flintstone with an angel over one shoulder and the devil over the other when he was faced with a dilemma. Fred was in the middle while the two of them tried to pull him in different directions. It was up to Fred to use his mind, heart, and soul to search for his truth. You are like Fred, and you always have that inner wisdom that knows the truth of what is right for you.

If you are busying yourself all the time and rushing from one event to the next, your truth gets lost in there somewhere, and you are just coasting on autopilot.

The purpose of meditating is to flex your intuition muscle. The more you meditate and sit with your divine self, the stronger the muscle. Through initiating your mindfulness and awareness in meditation, the more your true self can emerge, and you can respond to life rather than reacting to it.

Responding vs. Reacting

Our lives seem to be busier and busier and moving faster than we can think. We tend to react to life rather than responding to life. These are two entirely different behaviors. Reacting is a negative choice and not who we really are. Reactions are unconscious; there's little or no real thinking involved. As we mature and grow, it is imperative that we don't act on these temporary feelings and learn to practice self-control. Responding is using our intuition, who we really are: light, compassion, and love. The word *respond* has the same root as responsibility. Without taking responsibility for your actions, it will be hard to achieve anything in your life. So a response to an event or circumstance is much better than a reaction.

For example, a child spills a glass of milk onto the floor. If we have been busy all day, not taking any time for ourselves, we may react by yelling and getting angry, hurting the child's feelings, etc. It was most likely unintentional and an accident. Imagine it was you who spilled the milk; would you like to be talked to poorly or disrespected? Most likely not. Now, if we choose to respond, we can make sure everyone is okay, clean up the mess, and show the child where a better place might be to place the glass next time.

Since I am a big fan of football, I will use an example of a professional quarterback who is losing with five minutes left in the game. I have noticed that, when their teams are losing, some of the elite quarterbacks *respond* to the task at hand with ease, calm, and dignity. Passes are completed, the team is focused and centered, and the task is executed, while a quarterback who *reacts* to being behind is quick and erratic and forces the catches and plays. The team seems to be unsteady and not focused. Which quarterback would you want on your team? Which quarterback most likely leads his team to victory?

Meditation helps us respond to stress rather than react to stress. It calms the mind and keeps us centered and close to the root of who we truly are. It's a time to step back and slow down.

Religion

To me, religion and spirituality are not the same; they are complementary. I find it difficult to subscribe to one religion, just as I can't commit to one political party. Spirituality is a state of mind in which you are connected to your inner healer, your truth, which you can grasp at any time, but most likely in a quiet, still moment or when you are doing what you love. Religion has rules, stories, and sets of doctrines and beliefs that are different from religion to religion. I have nothing against religion; I attend Mass regularly and send my children to parochial school. I think it's good to search out different religions and find one that suits your beliefs. The religion you choose should make you feel welcome, supported, and inspired. For many, feeding their spirit happens in a mosque, church, synagogue, etc., and for others it happens during meditation or when swimming in a lake. Spirituality is a part of religion, so it's up to you if you want to express it through religious ceremonies and in places of worship. I think the problem that ails us if we attend service once a week is that we feel that that activity fills the spiritual hole and go on with our daily lives. Attending to the spirit should be a daily practice of at least five minutes. One hour a week usually doesn't cut it.

Service Feeds the Spirit

Another way to feed the spirit is to give to others. In helping others, you help yourself. When you are in service to others through charity work, donations, giving back to your community or a place that has helped you in the past like a school or a gym, you are connected to your soul. I like to do charity runs, volunteer at school and church, donate to causes close to my heart, and support friends with their philanthropic journeys. When we give to others, we bring light into our lives, which can then become happier and more peaceful. Look up some different charities with which you would like to get involved, and sign up for a race or volunteer. Give back in some way, and I promise your life will become richer. It's more or less impossible to be sad or depressed when you are giving your time and talent to someone/something in need.

Wide-Awake Reflection

Pull out your journal and brainstorm about some ways you can express your spirituality. Can you spend at least fifteen minutes a day in nature? Can you visit different churches and study different religions to see what suits for your current beliefs best? Commit to at least five minutes a day of meditating. Just be still with no distractions. Breathe. Keep breathing. You are doing great!

> *In the beginning, spirituality is a seeking practice. We seek peace, we seek joy, we seek wisdom, we seek awakening, we seek self-betterment. Farther down the road, the realization comes that we already are the peace and joy and wisdom and awakening and self-betterment that we seek. At that point, spirituality becomes what it is . . . Not a practice of seeking anything. A practice of uncovering what was there inside you all along. You already are the light at the end of the tunnel. You already are the wisdom, you already are the peace, you already are the joy. You already are awakened, you already are perfect. All that's left is for you to discover that you are.*
>
> –Teal Scott

IV

Connecting Mind, Body, and Spirit

CHAPTER 8

Healing Your Life through Chakra Balancing

Health is a large word. It embraces not the body only, but the mind and spirit as well . . . and not today's pain or pleasure alone, but the whole being and outlook of a man.
—James H. West

Emotion always has its roots in the unconscious and manifests itself in the body.
—Irene Claremont de Castillejo

I implore you to buy the book You Can Heal Your Life by Louise Hay. Ms. Hay has spent over thirty years doing research showing that if you do not deal with spiritual, emotional, mental, or physical issues, you are more likely to manifest a physical illness or disease in the body. Have you ever gotten a stomach ache before you had to speak in front of people or take a test? This is the mental stress physically manifesting itself. Deep down most of us know that there is a link between how we live our lives and our health.

What is ailing you? I couldn't figure out why I had an eating disorder but I knew I had one. Now I know that anorexia was just a symptom of my sense of unworthiness. I used to joke to my husband that dieting was the only thing I was good at. If there was a major for it, I took the A's home. It defined me and who I was. People came to me for a diet advice. Many wondered about my superpowered self-discipline! What they didn't know was how crazy my thoughts were and how royally depressed I was.

In Heal Your Life, Hay lists every ailment and/or disease and then gives the mental cause for each. For anorexia, this is what she states: "Denying the self life. Extreme fear, self-hatred, and rejection." That was me to the tenth degree. I hated living. My life was dismal, my emotions were angry, and I hated the thought of myself. I had to take the hard steps to control my life and find out who I really was, deep inside, and what I really wanted. It was time to grieve the loss of my mother and face it and accept the fact that she was never coming back. My whole body was off balance because my emotions were being pushed further and further down. I refused to face my emotions, so I distracted myself with restricting food. As the years went on, I became increasingly disconnected and angry. I was mad at the world, and my soul was dying because I felt there was no purpose to my life, and my physical life was dying too.

Chakra 101

Our body is made up of a series of atoms that have positive and negative energy charges. According to ancient yoga tradition rooted in Hinduism and Buddhism, chakras are the energy points in the body located along the spine extending from the top of skull to the base of the spinal column. There are a total of seven, according to most textbooks and research. Judith Anodea, author of *Wheels of Life: A User's Guide to the Chakra System*, defines a chakra this way: "A chakra is believed to be a center of activity that receives, assimilates, and expresses life force energy." Chakras are energetic fields that are connected to every organ in our bodies. The seven chakras are said to bring in healing energy to keep our bodies, spirits, and minds in balance. According to Dr. Deepak Chopra, "Chakras govern the core emotional and physical functions of your being. When these centers are congested or out of harmony, your vital life energy is unable to freely circulate, resulting in distress, disease, and lack of mind-body integrity." I love this idea of your body mirroring what is going on in your mind. How does an anorexic really look? He or she looks starved, lonely, lost, confused, and sad. Our bodies hear what we are feeling and saying to ourselves. Do you see how the mind and body might be connected?

Each chakra is associated with certain organs in the body. Positive energy through our thoughts, feelings, and actions allows the organ to function properly. If there are any disturbances through negative thoughts, poor diet, and/or a harmful emotional environment, the chakra goes off balance and can wreak havoc on the body through illness, infection, disease, etc. For example, if someone suffers a heart attack, the heart chakra is off balance. For this person, they may be having love or relationship issues, lack of self-control as far as what they are eating, or trouble accepting who they really are. In my case, anorexia affected the whole body—all the chakras. My kidneys were not working well, my digestive organs were tired, and my skin, hair, and nails were brittle and coarse.

As we go through each chakra, we can gain greater insight into what our body is telling us, what thoughts and past emotions we need to release, and how we can heal the body to get it working synergistically again. Think about what is presently ailing you. What is anorexia doing to your body? Do you experience stomach pains? Do you have mouth sores? Do you have anemia, osteoporosis, constipation, or bloating? Many of these symptoms are rooted in a certain chakra. For example, mouth sores are located in the throat chakra. Focus on healing the throat chakra with the healing plan I have provided for you within that chakra. Since anorexia deals with every chakra, it's very important to go through each chakra carefully and identify the emotional blocks in each one. Eating disorders are rooted in the first chakra. If the first chakra is off balance, it affects all the chakras.

The body is constantly working to balance us. All parts of the equation (Body + Mind + Spirit = Balanced Whole) need to be balanced for us to feel fully awake, alive, and in love with life. There are always things to improve on, as we have been put on this earth to live out our purpose, and that requires learning and growing!

I will explain each chakra, its symbol, its corresponding organs, poses to release deep emotional pain, restoring techniques, healing foods and oils, and the thought or affirmation to work on as you recharge your chakra. With the yoga poses, I will give you step-by-step instructions about how to get into the pose. Don't worry if you have never done yoga before. Just keep an open mind and be gentle with yourself.

You will be able to identify which chakras are blocked by some of the physical ailments you are experiencing. I have come up with my own Wide-Awakening Healing Plan to help you increase the energy centers that are off balance. You can cure the ailment if you practice the Wide-Awake Plan laid out for you. Your mind is very powerful and beautiful! There also will be other suggestions for each chakra healing pertaining to the colors you wear, the colors you use in your home, the music you listen to, and exercise you engage in.

Chakra energy healing will create the harmony you deserve between the body, mind, and spirit.

Chakra 1: Root Chakra—To be secure/safe

The root chakra is our life-force energy. It governs the connection to your existence and why you are here. It is where your most organic power began. Your existence is enough as is. Your sense of belonging is secure. The root chakra is located at the base of your spine at the coccyx bone. It radiates the color red. Red is the color of the life force and represents passion and courage. Its function relates to your basic instinct of survival, support, grounding, and courage. If open, our lives feel constant, stable, and secure. This chakra represents your individuality and how you express it.

This energy center will function properly when you feel secure and safe in your physical self by knowing who you really are and not being influenced by others' behaviors. You have magnetic energy and radiate self-confidence. You can handle what life serves you and live with conviction as you stand up for yourself to pursue what's best for your life. If you are busy fulfilling societal or family expectations about what you should be doing, this chakra becomes imbalanced. You will notice this imbalance as you feel the need to control everything and everyone, are quick to react in anger, and feel stress and anxiety throughout the day. This imbalance will eventually lead to an imbalance in the body as well.

Body parts affected by a first-chakra imbalance

Spine, Large Intestine, Legs, Bladder, Feet, Blood, Bones, Tailbone, Circulation

Are you noticing any level of discomfort, pain, bleeding, disease, illness in any of these organs? If you are, this chakra may need to be rebalanced/unblocked.

Physical dis-ease manifestation

Eating disorders, Blood disorders, Irritable bowel/Hemorrhoids/Constipation, Colds, Body temperature irregularity, Back issues, Depression/Bipolar disorder, Cancer of the first chakra organs

Wide-Awake Chakra Balancing Plan

1. Meditative Relaxation

Find a place where it is calm, uncluttered, and full of positive energy to practice your chakra healing. Start out by taking in a few deep breaths while seated in a comfortable position. Exhaling through the mouth and inhaling through the nose. Your brain can't function properly unless your breath is even and relaxed, so center yourself and focus on the breath. Focus on the base of your spine where this energy is located. The color that vibrates in the root chakra is red. Imagine a spinning red wheel at the base of your spine and feel energy radiate to that place. Feel light enter your physical being. Breathe into the light. Imagine it radiating through the lower part of your spine. Relax here for at least five minutes, giving your mind, body, and spirit the attention they need and love.

2. Yoga Poses

(a) *Mountain pose*. This is one of the most basic poses in yoga but one of the most important. It's a grounding exercise to feel connected to the earth and your body, and it is very calming to the body and mind. Standing barefoot on a mat, the earth, or wherever it feels most comfortable to you, stand up tall with your shoulders back and neck relaxed, arms to the side. Spread your toes wide and lift them off the mat to regain your sense of balance, strength, and connection to your soul. Chin is lifted. You will begin to feel the sense of strength in this pose as you rest comfortably in it. Stand in the glory of all that is you. Beautiful, radiant you! Hold this position for ten deep breaths.

(b) *Bridge pose*. Another grounding pose that brings awareness to your connection to the earth and helps you feel safe in your physical body is bridge pose. In a lying position, bring your knees up toward your chest, bringing your heels close to your body, extending your arms and using your fingertips to touch the heels lightly. Raise your bottom and lift slowly off the floor, rooting your feet to the earth. Feel a strong connection to the ground and hold the pose for one minute. Let your body feel the sensation of the strength that lies within you.

(c) *Standing forward bend.* In a standing position, bring your legs together and let your chin drop to your chest. Now bring yourself forward, bending at the waist, one vertebra at a time, and let your arms go. If you can reach the ground with your fingers, do so. If you can bring your nose to your knees, do so. There is no judgment here. Let your body relax with even breaths and flow. Let your mind go. Stay in this position for five deep breaths.

3. Journaling

This is where the meditation, yoga, and your thoughts come together. In balancing this chakra, childhood hurts will be revealed. Is there something or someone you have not forgiven from your childhood? Have you forgiven yourself? Did they tell you that you couldn't do something? Did they not support your efforts to live out your dreams? Journal the events that have given you pain. Revisit the pain we discussed in chapter 1. Release the pain to the universe. Forgive the ones who hurt you. In truth, they were only doing the best they could with the resources they had. You can heal this hurt and heal your past. Next, write down all that you love to do, your passions. Be sure to set some time every day to pursue what you love. It's your birthright.

> *And remember, no matter where you go, there you are.*
> –Confucius

4. Healing Foods

Since red is the color for this chakra, you should be incorporating more red foods into your diet. For example, beets, radishes, and cayenne pepper, are all good choices. Incorporate more red drinks into your diet as well.

5. Healing Activities

Physical activity; deep, peaceful sleep; more red clothing, Latin American music with deep, strong beats.

Wide-Awake Affirmation

I am safe with who I am. My life has meaning. I will use my talents to serve my purpose. I am protected and secure.

Second Chakra: Sacral Chakra—To feel/express

The sacral chakra is the center of emotions and desires. Yes, this is about all those emotions. It relates to how you handle and express your emotions, how you live in the present moment, and how you handle sexual energy and intimacy. How are your personal relationships? Are you emotionally connected? Are you enjoying life? Do you feel bonds with your family, friends, and community? This chakra is located between the navel and the pubic bone, and it radiates the color orange. Orange represents sensuality, sexuality, joy, and compassion.

When functioning properly, the sacral chakra will allow you to express your emotions honestly and openly. You feel safe to express yourself to your friends and family. You stay true to who you are. You feel safe in the physical home of your soul—the body—which allows you be intimate without reservation, take pleasure in the senses, and be comfortable with your sexuality. If it becomes blocked, you can become disconnected from romantic partners and may become sexually dysfunctional; you may become shy; and you can experience trust issues with others.

Body parts affected by a second-chakra imbalance

Reproductive organs, Stomach, Liver, Gallbladder, Pancreas, Kidneys

Are you noticing any level of discomfort, pain, bleeding, disease, illness in any of these organs? If you are, this chakra may need to be rebalanced/unblocked.

Physical dis-ease manifestation

Low libido, Hormonal imbalances/Menstruation issues, Cancer of the second chakra organs, Digestive disorders, Urinary dysfunction, Eating disorders, Depression

Wide-Awake Chakra Balancing Plan

1. Meditative Relaxation

Find a place that is calm, uncluttered, and full of positive energy to practice your chakra healing. Start out by taking a few deep breaths while seated in a comfortable position. Exhaling through the mouth and inhaling through the nose. Your brain can't function properly unless your breath is even and relaxed. Focus on the space between your belly button and your sex organs. The color that vibrates in the sacral chakra is orange. Imagine a spinning orange wheel below your navel, and feel energy radiate from that space. Feel light enter your physical being. Relax here for at least five minutes, giving your mind, body, and spirit the attention they need and love.

2. Yoga Poses

(a) *Bound angle pose.* In a seated position, bring the bottoms of your feet together in front of you. Place your hands on your feet. Sit up tall and stretch your knees toward the opposite sides of the room. Take five long, deep breaths, breathing into the space below your navel. You will feel an opening at your groin muscles. You will feel tension and stress release as you get deeper into the pose. This is a great hip opener.

(b) *Low squat pose.* Squat down with your feet flat on the floor. Let your body weight go, but keep your bottom off the ground, hovering into a squatting position. You can rest your elbows inside the knees or wherever your arms feel most comfortable. Relax into the pose for five deep breaths. Keep looking straight ahead, and focus on releasing tension in the sacral area.

(c) *Wide-angle seated forward bend.* In a seated position, spread your legs open wide, extending them toward the sides of the room. Fold forward, slowly and gently, feeling a slight pull in the groin area. Stretch to where you feel a comfortable tug. Rest in the pose with five full, deep breaths, being gentle with your thoughts.

3. Journaling

In this journal entry, write about your relationships with your mother and father and your significant other. Journal about ways you can nurture your relationships with the ones you love the most. Is it forgiveness? Compromise? Do you need to set new, clear boundaries? Are you in a relationship that no longer serves you? This is your life now. *You* make the choices about who you want to be a part of your life. If sexual abuse has occurred in your life, get the anger, hurt, and fear on paper and forgive that person—I know it's hard, and I didn't say condone the act or let the person into your life—for your benefit, and give yourself all the love you deserve. *Let it go.* If you can't seem to get past the event, the pain and hurt of it all, confide in a trusted friend or family member and/or licensed therapist. You can heal your past and the relationships that were difficult.

> *Never apologize for showing feeling. When you do so, you apologize for the truth.*
> —Benjamin Disraeli

4. Healing Foods

Eat healthy oils like coconut and olive, EFAs from fish, nuts, and seeds, and any orange-colored foods like salmon, apricot, papaya, yams, and oranges. Orange drinks will reenergize as well. Maca powder (sold in health food stores) is a great addition to balance this chakra

5. Healing Activities

Take hot baths; wear orange clothes, scarves, and jewelry; have a gentle massage; focus on feeling with your five senses when engaging in any activity. Remember, this is the feeling chakra, so your goal is to feel as much as possible.

Wide-Awake Affirmation

I am here in the present moment. I enjoy a healthy, fulfilling life. I am sensual. My relationships enrich my life.

Third Chakra: Solar Plexus Chakra—To be self-assured

The third chakra is all about your personal power, your sense of self-worth, and feeling that you are "enough." Yep, that self-esteem thing we've been talking about! The solar plexus chakra, when functioning properly, allows you to feel confident in who you are and to possess a strong sense of self-worth. You do not hide your gifts and talents from the world. You are immune to critics and do not feel the need to control any aspect of your life. You feel empowered, strong, and open to fresh, new ideas. You stay focused on what's important to you, despite criticism from others. Your dreams and goals become reality! To stay balanced, keep focused on what you want for your life, and the chakra will remain open. This chakra radiates the color yellow and is located at the navel. Yellow gives the spirit life and hope with ease. We honor who we really are.

When the third chakra is imbalanced or blocked, you experience anger, fear, and resentment, and you need more power often. You feel like you are never enough and are quite needy in relation to your loved ones. You worry a lot and feel nervous and hungry very often. You listen to others' opinions more than your own and are not true to what you know and love. Your personal power becomes compromised. Have no fear; you can rebalance this! Let's do the work, shall we?

Body parts affected by a third-chakra imbalance

Digestive system, Kidney, Pancreas, Stomach, Liver, Colon, Spleen, Small intestines

Are you noticing any level of discomfort, pain, bleeding, disease, illness in any of these organs? If you are, this chakra may need to be rebalanced/unblocked.

Physical dis-ease manifestation

Eating disorders, Ulcers and Gallstones, Kidney disease, Arthritis, Cancer of the digestive organs, Diabetes, Hepatitis

Wide-Awake Chakra Balancing Plan

1. Meditative Relaxation

Find a place that is calm, uncluttered, and full of positive energy to practice your chakra healing. Start out by taking in a few deep breaths while seated in a comfortable position. Exhaling through the mouth and inhaling through the nose. Your brain can't function properly unless your breath is even and relaxed. Focus on the space around your navel. The color that vibrates in the sacral chakra is orange. Imagine a spinning yellow wheel at your navel, and feel energy radiate to that space. Feel light enter your physical being. Relax here for at least five minutes, giving your mind, body, and spirit the attention they need and love.

2. Yoga Poses

(a) *Bow pose.* Lying on your stomach, lift your chin off the floor and reach one arm back to the leg on the same side, one at a time. Try to grab your ankles while lifting your chest off the floor. Hold for three inhales and exhales. Take yourself down slowly.

(b) *Standing split pose.* Stand tall and relaxed, and bend over into a standing forward fold (from the root chakra). Lift the right leg while balancing yourself, both hands on the floor. Root your left leg into the floor while the right leg reaches behind you or up to the ceiling. Hold for five deep breaths. Switch legs and hold for five deep breaths.

(c) *Boat pose.* Sit on your mat, legs extended in front of you. Lean your body back while lifting your legs off the mat. You are now balancing on your tailbone. Do not round or arch the back, but keep yourself straight yet relaxed. Variations are to bend at the knee and hold the backs of the calves with your hands or to stretch the legs out long and straight in front of you. Strengthening your core muscles gives power back to the third chakra.

3. Journaling

While journaling about this blockage/imbalance, I want you to answer these questions: What do you do in your spare time when you feel the most at peace with yourself? Is it dancing, singing, art, making jewelry? Are you struggling to find your life's purpose, your calling? What's holding you back from taking that leap of faith? You—and only you—determine your life's journey. What makes your heart happy? Do you like playing with kids? List all the things you *love* to do. Let it flow onto the paper. Build up the courage to be yourself, and don't let anyone or anything stop you. You are enough as is. You were born with the gift of being you. There is no one else like you on this Earth.

> *Your time is limited, so don't waste it living someone else's life. Don't be trapped by dogma, which is living with the results of other people's thinking. Don't let the noise of others' opinions drown out your own inner voice. Most important, have the courage to follow your heart and intuition.*
> —Steve Jobs

> *It is not the mountain we conquer but ourselves.*
> —Edmund Hillary

4. Healing Foods

Yellow foods are important to eat to heal this blockage. Corn, yellow bell peppers, and squash are great choices. Whole wheat, sprouted grains, and soothing teas, such as peppermint and chamomile work well too. Also be sure to include yellow-colored beverages.

5. Healing Third-Chakra Activities

Get creative through arts like painting, drawing, photography, crafts, or playing a musical instrument. Listen to music with soothing chimes. Engage in core-boosting physical activity such as Pilates, weight training, ice-skating, skiing, tennis, basketball, etc.

Wide-Awake Affirmation

I love and honor myself. My choices are my responsibility and no one else's. I feel happy when pursuing my deepest passions.

Fourth Chakra: Heart Chakra—To give and receive love

The heart chakra represents our ability to love others and ourselves, show compassion and empathy, and forgive others. You share your love effortlessly with many if your heart chakra is balanced. The key issue is unconditional love for yourself and your loved ones. Forgiveness, including self-forgiveness, is a big theme here. Are you having a hard time forgiving yourself for your mistakes? Show some self-compassion. Your mistakes are stepping-stones toward getting better. Furthermore, is there someone you need to forgive? Can you show some compassion to that person by seeing that they were doing the best they could with what they know?

The location of the heart chakra, is—yes, you guessed it—the heart, the center of the chest. This chakra radiates the color green.

When the heart chakra is functioning properly, you are able to receive love and show it, too. Your close relationships feel connected, you forgive easily, and you show compassion for yourself and others. An imbalanced heart chakra causes you to feel jealousy, anger, the desire for revenge, and a lack of empathy for others. You may seem cold and distant.

Body parts affected by a heart-chakra imbalance

Heart, Breasts, Lungs

Are you noticing any level of pain, bleeding, disease, or illness in any of these organs? If you are, this chakra may need to be rebalanced/unblocked.

Physical dis-ease manifestation

Heart diseases, Hypertension, Asthma, Cancer of heart-chakra organs, Allergies, Cystic fibrosis, Emphysema, Pulmonary diseases

Wide-Awake Chakra Balancing Plan

1. Meditative Relaxation

Find a place that is calm, uncluttered, and full of positive energy to practice your chakra healing. Start out by taking in a few deep breaths while seated in a comfortable position. Exhaling through the mouth and inhaling through the nose. Your brain can't function properly unless your breath is even and relaxed. Focus on the space at the center of your chest. The color that vibrates in the heart chakra is green. Imagine a spinning green wheel in your chest and feel energy radiate to that space. Feel light enter your physical being. Relax for at least five minutes, giving your mind, body, and spirit the attention they need and love.

2. Yoga Poses

(a) *Camel pose.* Resting on the mat on your knees, open your chest and allow your arms to fall to the sides of your body. If you can reach further, grab your ankles with both hands, keeping chest open, head and chin relaxed, and breathing smoothly. Bring your hips forward and keep your throat open. Hold for three deep breaths.

(b) *Cobra pose.* Lying on your stomach on the mat, place your hands on the outsides of your ribs. Lifting your chest while straightening your arms, arch back slightly, opening your chest. Take five deep breaths, in through the nose and out through the mouth.

(c) *Cow.* Bring yourself onto all fours on the mat with hips square, shoulders over arms, knees below hips. Slowly lift your chin up while lifting your tailbone, arching the back gently. Let your belly drop toward the mat, keeping your chest open to the front of the room. Hold for three deep breaths.

3. Journaling

If we are constantly looking outside of ourselves to create a feeling of happiness, we will never be content. We must love ourselves first, in order to extend that to other people, animals, the earth, and life. Make a list in your journal of the wonderful qualities you possess. If you are in a dark space and cannot come up with these, recall times when others have complimented you on your giving heart, your loving words, or your sensitive spirit. Write down those compliments even if you do not believe them. As we choose love, we also choose life. The essence of your being is love. Choose love over fear, and get to the heart of your natural state.

> *Love is energy: it can neither be created nor destroyed. It just is and always will be, giving meaning to life and direction to goodness... Love will never die.*
> —Bryce Courtney

> *When your heart speaks, take good notes.*
> —Judith Campbell

4. Healing Foods

Eating and drinking green foods helps balance the heart chakra. Try broccoli, spinach, kale, leafy greens, and green tea. Green herbs such as parsley, basil, and cilantro are great additions to your cooking as well.

5. Healing Activities

The following are activities that can heal the heart chakra: nature walks; quality time with family and friends; wearing green clothing, jewelry, and scarves; listening to nature sounds or music; growing plants, flowers or a garden; watching romantic movies.

Wide-Awake Affirmation

I am loving. I am loved. I love myself. I am love.

Fifth Chakra: Throat Chakra—To speak

The throat chakra represents our self-expression—the need to be "heard"—and communicating our needs effectively. With a balanced throat chakra, we are able to communicate our passions with great ease and natural authority and find true joy in doing so. This chakra also focuses on the ability to trust and to remain loyal. Money issues are rooted in this chakra as well. The throat chakra lies all along the throat region and radiates a light-blue color.

Do you express yourself freely and voice your opinions effectively? Do you trust others without doubting their intentions? Are you financially secure and responsible with your money? When the throat chakra is functioning properly, you can clearly and openly express yourself to others. Your truth is spoken. You handle your earnings effectively and efficiently without overspending. You organize your finances in a way that is responsible. If you throat chakra is imbalanced you may become dishonest and more likely to criticize others. Fear of speaking up is a major indication that your throat chakra is out of whack. Stifling your inner voice causes this chakra to become imbalanced or blocked.

Body parts affected by fifth-chakra imbalance

Mouth, Teeth, Tongue, Glands, Jaw, Ears, Neck, Shoulders, Throat

Are you noticing any level of pain, bleeding, disease, or illness in any of these organs? If you are, this chakra may need to be rebalanced/unblocked.

Physical dis-ease manifestation

Thyroid disorders, Mouth issues like tooth decay, gingivitis, root canals, or TMJ, Cancer of throat chakra organs, Hormonal issues related to PMS, Ear infections, earaches, hearing problems, deafness

Wide-Awake Chakra Balancing Plan

1. Meditative Relaxation

Find a place that is calm, uncluttered, and full of positive energy to practice your chakra healing. Start out by taking in a few deep breaths while seated in a comfortable position. Exhaling through the mouth and inhaling through the nose. Your brain can't function properly unless your breath is even and relaxed. Focus on the space in middle of your throat. The color that vibrates in the throat chakra is blue. Imagine a spinning blue wheel in your chest and feel energy radiate to that space. Feel light enter your physical being. Relax here for at least five minutes, giving your mind, body, and spirit the attention they need and love.

2. Yoga Poses

(a) *Bridge pose.* Lying on your back on the mat, slowly peel your lower back off the mat, lifting one vertebra at a time. Keeping your head, neck, and shoulders on the mat and chin lifted, squeeze your buttocks together at the top of the pose. Be sure to breathe evenly, taking five deep breaths in the pose.

(b) *Supported shoulder stand.* Lying on your back, arms outstretched to either side, slowly lift your legs straight above you. Bringing your arms and hands to support your tailbone, you should feel your chest rise gently toward your throat. Hold the pose for three deep breaths. Bring yourself down slowly and gently.

(c) *Fish pose*. Lie on your back on the mat. Slowly bring the top of your head to the mat by releasing your neck and throat to the ceiling. Your arms will be supporting you while you come up on your elbows. Give yourself some time to work into this pose. Slowly come out of it by pressing your forearms into the mat and gently bringing your head up and off the mat. Lower yourself gently.

3. Journaling

Ask yourself what you are holding back from telling someone. Can you speak your truth with love? Are you afraid of criticism? Write down a dialogue in your journal of what you want to tell the people to whom you have not spoken your truth. This will help take the emotion out of it. You will be prepared, calm, and focused. No matter what you do, you will be criticized by someone. We are all unique. Continue to be yourself. The ones who support you and love you unconditionally will stay in your life. They will listen and consider your requests and feelings.

> *The eloquent man is he who is no beautiful speaker, but who is inwardly and desperately drunk with a certain belief.*
> —Ralph Waldo Emerson

4. Healing Foods

To unblock the throat chakra, many liquids should be consumed. Water, teas, and light fruit juices are good choices. Soup is wonderful to open the throat chakra. You want to keep the throat open and hydrated. Spice up your water or tea with a few lemons too!

5. Healing Activities

The following activities will help heal the throat chakra: singing; wearing blue clothing and jewelry; neck and shoulder massages; repetitive music such as ocean waves, echoing sounds, or soft, spiritual tones; attending self-development courses and seminars; and spending time in a religious or spiritual building.

Wide-Awake Affirmation

I will speak my truth. I am secure in what I know and what I want. I trust others and do not question their intentions.

Sixth Chakra: The Third-Eye Chakra—To see

The third-eye chakra or brow chakra represents our intuition, wisdom, and intelligence. When it is open and balanced, you trust your intuition and insights about life. You think for yourself and rely on your inner knowledge about your life's direction, but you remain open-minded. It connects us to the wisdom within. This chakra is located midway between the brows at the center of the forehead. The color it radiates is a deep-blue or indigo. Many people refer to it as the mind's eye because this is where your mind sees and knows the truth.

When the third-eye chakra is functioning properly, you follow your life's purpose. You have the wisdom to know that you make a difference in this world by using the gifts and talents that are unique to you. If this chakra becomes imbalanced, you may fantasize too much and become stuck in one rigid belief system and not keep an open mind about others' beliefs. Depression is very common with a blocked sixth chakra. This imbalance can make you feel lonely and depressed, sometimes aggressive and confused.

Body parts affected by third-eye chakra imbalance

Brain
Eyes
Nose
Sinuses
Face

Are you noticing any level of discomfort, pain, bleeding, disease, illness in any of these organs? If you are, this chakra may need to be rebalanced/unblocked.

Physical dis-ease manifestation

Blindness, Cancer of the third-eye chakra organs, Strokes, Migraines, Dementia, Eye problems, Depression

Wide-Awake Chakra Balancing Plan

1. Meditative Relaxation

Find a place that is calm, uncluttered, and full of positive energy to practice your chakra healing. Start out by taking in a few deep breaths while seated in a comfortable position. Exhaling through the mouth and inhaling through the nose. Your brain can't function properly unless your breath is even and relaxed. Focus on the space between your eyebrows and slightly above. The color that vibrates in the third-eye chakra is purple. Imagine a spinning purple wheel in between your eyes, and feel energy radiate to that space. Feel light enter your physical being. Relax for at least five minutes, giving your mind, body, and spirit the attention they need and love.

2.Yoga Poses

(a) *Child's pose*. Bring yourself up onto all fours—shoulders over wrists, belly pulled in, back in alignment, and hips over knees. Lower your lower back so that it rests on the backs of your calves. Draw your forehead to the mat while reaching your arms overhead. Take five deep breaths, drawing breath in through your nose and out through the mouth. Take it slow, and let your body release. Massage your third eye gently by rolling your forehead side to side, up and down, to stimulate the flow.

(b) *Dolphin pose*. From a standing position extend into a forward fold position. Fingers should be interlaced. Your elbows should be directly beneath your shoulders. Your head should be on the mat, your hands touching your head. Be careful not to hurt your neck. Bring your legs as close to your head as possible. If you are a more advanced yogi, take the position into a handstand or a headstand to deepen your practice.

(c) *Yoga mudra*. This a position usually performed solely with your hands and fingers, which seals and directs energy through the body. It's a very powerful way of drawing energy to parts of the body that need our attention and love. It's like speaking to the body without words. How you hold your hands and position your fingers in a given posture will generate different energies and reactions to those energies. For this specific exercise, we will be sitting cross-legged, body upright, chest lifted, and eyes closed. Bringing your palms together in prayer position, lift your hands to the space between your brows, and honor your divine wisdom with ten deep breaths, inhaling through the nose and exhaling through the mouth. Make peace with your intuition, and let it guide you. Your mind is all-knowing.

3. Journaling

Ask yourself in this part of your healing to call on your soul. The part of you that feels, hears, and loves you unconditionally and truthfully. Stop relying on others to make decisions. Your intuition can be trusted. You are open and receiving information from your Self every day. Write down in your journal a decision you need to make. Let your pen guide you and your mind flow. Breathe. Break the decision into a table of pros on one side and cons on the other. Which column outweighs the other? Do them. Life will change when you start listening to your intuition. Think of your future as beautiful, successful, and full of many blessings.

> *Trust your own instinct. Your mistakes might as well be your own, instead of someone else's.*
>
> –Billy Wilder

4. Healing Foods

Dark-blue or red fruits like blackberries, grapes, and raspberries stimulate the third-eye chakra. Any alcohol can be enjoyed, but especially red wine. Chocolate is also a great stimulator.

5. Healing Activities

Daydreaming, meditation, listening to classical music, chanting, and stargazing are healing to the third-eye chakra.

Wide-Awake Affirmation

I follow my intuition. I trust myself and am all-knowing.

Seventh Chakra: Crown Chakra—To know

The crown chakra represents our inner peace, enlightenment, selflessness, humanitarianism, and faith in the universe or a higher power. When the crown chakra is balanced, you have attained peace with a higher power and the universe. You will feel inner peace and connected to something bigger than all this. Your creator is a big part of your life. A balanced crown chakra allows you to know that there is more to life than just the physical world and enables you to see beyond it with an open mind. The crown chakra allows wisdom to flow to us effortlessly. Synchronicity plays a role here. Miracles occur in your life, and coincidences happen regularly.

At conception, we are birthed as a soul. We are light, energy, and love at this time. The heart starts beating about eighteen days after conception. Our physical bodies are not completely formed until eight weeks after conception. So you see, our physical bodies enable us to express our souls here on earth. Your soul is who you are; it's loving, kind, radiant, bursting with light. The physical body allows your soul to do the work on this planet, whether it's making jewelry or being a stay-at-home mom caring for your baby or running a company that makes computers so you can make others' lives easier with technology. You *have* a body, but you *are* a soul. If the crown chakra is imbalanced, you may lack understanding of your role in the world and become mentally confused, depressed, and neurotic.

Body parts associated with the crown chakra

Brain, Head

Are you noticing any level of pain, bleeding, disease, or illness in any of these organs? If you are, this chakra may need to be rebalanced/unblocked.

Physical dis-ease manifestation

Depression, senility, Mental illnesses, Coordination problems, Schizophrenia, Baldness, Lack of mental clarity/cloudiness, Epilepsy

Wide-Awake Chakra Balancing Plan

1. Meditative Relaxation

Find a place that is calm, uncluttered, and full of positive energy to practice your chakra healing. Start out by taking in a few deep breaths while seated in a comfortable position. Exhaling through the mouth and inhaling through the nose. Your brain can't function properly unless your breath is even and relaxed. Focus on the space between your eyebrows and slightly above. The color that vibrates in the crown chakra is purple. Imagine a spinning purple wheel in between your eyes, and feel energy radiate to that space. Feel Light enter your physical being. Relax here for at least five minutes, giving your mind, body, and spirit the attention they need and love.

2. Yoga poses

(a) *Corpse pose.* If you have ever been to a yoga class, you may have experienced corpse pose. It is the position you enter at the conclusion of the class. To get into corpse pose, you will lie on your back on the floor. Your arms and legs are completely relaxed, your arms stretched alongside your body with palms facing up. You should feel calm and completely comfortable. Spend five to ten minutes in this pose after you have performed your spiritual movement of choice. Make sure you are breathing deeply and peacefully. Give your body and mind the break they deserve.

(b) *Half-lotus pose.* Most of us are familiar with the phrase "Criss-cross, applesauce," which we learned in preschool. This position also looks like the typical pose used for meditation. Sit up tall. Cross your legs over one another in front of you. Both knees should be resting out in front of you so your spine is straight. Your hands can be in prayer position in front of the heart or resting on the tops of your knees, palms facing up.

(c) *Legs-up-the-wall pose.* Sit sideways and very close to the wall, one hip against the wall. Swing your legs up against the wall. Lie back gently. You may need to adjust by scooting your bottom toward the baseboard. If your hamstrings are tight, move out farther from the wall. A scented eye pillow is helpful to use here. Relax in this pose for as long a deep relaxation as you would like. This is the "grandfather of all restorative yoga poses."

3. Journaling

Surrender your worries to whomever will listen. Get still, get quiet! Find a physical space in your home or surroundings where you feel 100 percent comfortable, at ease, and calm and where it is completely quiet. For me, it's in nature. I love the mountains. Its quiet up there, and it is just you and God's creation spending some quality time together. Surrender your worries on paper to whomever you speak to. Then, believe everything will work out exactly as it should. It will be divine timing. Set aside a quiet time daily to ask for guidance regarding questions to which you may need the answers. The answers may not come right away, but keep practicing your "quiet time" on a daily basis.

> *It is only when we silent the blaring sounds of our daily existence that we can finally hear the whispers of truth that life reveals to us, as it stands knocking on the doorsteps of our hearts.*
> —K. T. Jong

4. Healing Foods

Purple foods such as grapes, blackberries, eggplant and any purple drinks like grape juices are healing for the crown chakra. Whole, organic, earth foods can be consumed here.

5. Healing Activities

Meditation, prayer, spiritual practices, and attending religious ceremonies are very healing. Restorative practices like tai chi and kundalini yoga are also helpful. Wear purple clothes and jewelry. White clothing can also be worn here. Guided meditations may be helpful too as you begin your healing journey.

Wide-Awake Affirmation

I understand the divine meaning in life. I am connected to a higher source. I am one with my source.

As you work on the chakra(s) that are imbalanced and nurture or maintain the ones that are balanced, many of the ailments you experience may go away. Depression may subside. Weight may stabilize to your body's optimal weight set point where you feel healthy, strong, and vibrant. Your body will work as a harmonious whole and maintain its balance. I don't want to get all woo-woo with you, but you may feel euphoric, as though a supernatural feeling has come over you. You are mindfully present in the moment you are in, and your energy vibration is strong, and only good things can come to you. You are in tune with your spirit/soul/the light in you and can only express love, as you have released a lot of pain and suffering through your chakra healing. Your body becomes the catalyst for your soul to express itself fully.

Did ya get that? In essence, practicing chakra healing will allow perfect health to be restored, and life will feel rich and full again! Happy healing!

Wide-Awake Reflection

In this chapter, we studied the energy points in the body and where we are holding our emotions. Focus for the next twenty-eight days on what you are holding back. For full recovery, you will need to work on all the chakras, but right now let's focus on what is ailing you presently. Where in the body is it located? Another approach is, if you are taking medicine, what part of the body is it treating? Is it your heart, your thyroid, or your mind (depression)? Go to that body part, give it love, talk to it as you would to a sad child, encourage it, practice the yoga poses, participate in some healing activities, and use the affirmations. Commit to the entire twenty-eight days. Small shifts will occur if you stay consistent and focused, and health will be restored. Then go to yoga class regularly, as it rebalances all the chakras. Try it!

CHAPTER

Fulfilling Your Passion, Living Your Purpose, and Experiencing Joy!

> *That music that you hear inside of you urging you to take risks and follow your dreams is your intuitive connection to the purpose in your heart since birth. Be enthusiastic about all that you do. Have that passion with the awareness that the word enthusiasm literally means "the God (enthos) within (iasm)." Don't die with your music still in you.*
>
> –Wayne Dyer

We made it. We are here. You are making great progress in your healing. You are not sweating the small stuff of cellulite and the too many bites of sweets through not engaging in silly diet trends, restriction, or strict dieting. We have learned to get quiet and still. We have moved our bodies in ways to open up and live with a greater intensity and passion, and now it's time to connect all the dots!

Shine, you beautiful soul, you!

We are all meant to fulfill our life's destiny. We learn fear from society, the media, and our upbringing. We are not meant to live in depression, loneliness, and fear as we do if we suffer from anorexia.

Repeat after me, "I will pursue my passion." Many people go through their whole lives having a dream inside of them that they never realize. They come up with a host of excuses that serve to delay what they are truly longing for.

I was recently listening to a radio show hosted by a pastor named Michael Bernhard Beckwith, who was explaining that there are three types of people in this world. I had to listen further to see what type of person I am. I thought there were only Type A and Type B. Well, my Type A personality just *had* to hear what this was all about . . . Michael Bernard Beckwith, minister and author of several books, and can be seen in the movie *The Secret*, hosts a beautiful and inspiring radio show to help people transform themselves and heal their lives. During his show he talked about the three types of people who live in our world:

1. Task-oriented people

These people go about their days performing daily tasks. Brushing their teeth, walking the dog, making their meals, filling up the car with gas, grocery shopping, going to their jobs and completing the assigned tasks, watching TV, and then going off to bed. You know, the day-to-day errands. They get things done, and yes, they get to cross things off their to-do list, but are they really happy? Beckwith claims that 90 percent aren't.

2. Goal-Oriented People

This person will complete several different tasks to achieve a goal. They feel they have a purpose, as they are plugging away at their to-do list to achieve that goal, but there is not much enthusiasm behind it. For example, a person who just goes in to that job every day, just to get "that paycheck." They are completing the daily tasks at their job, but really, when they leave for the day, are they fulfilled?

3. Purpose-Oriented People

These people pursue their passions. They choose love over fear and don't make excuses. They feel a deep sense of purpose to give back to the world. They follow their hearts by using their God-given talents. They *listen* to their hearts—to the inner wisdom that tells them to serve. They infuse inspiration into a room by their zest for life and their passion for their life's work. You've seen these people . . . they are the ones who greet you with a smile and are excited to be living out their dreams. Like your personal trainer who loves to talk biomechanics or nutrition. Then there are people who are not sorry that they love to paint or make jewelry or fix watches. They know they have a talent, a gift, that can help another person's life become easier and happier.

Every one of us is called to this Earth to fill our life's purpose. This purpose is unique to each and every one of us. All seven billion of us!

I have been all three of these types of people.

I was a task person until college, just plugging away at the day-to-day grind and not really conscious of my thoughts, actions, and purpose.

When I got to college, I was forced to create a goal and become that goal-oriented person. Well, declare a major, if you will. I thought, "Okay, I want to be a fashion designer. That's it—I like clothes, I love to dress people, so that's it!" Well, after one sewing class, I dropped that major ASAP! Then I decided on Hotel and Restaurant Management because it was fun, I'm a people person, and I liked to plan parties and host events. Really? Hmmmmm . . . I really had no idea what I wanted to do because I was suffering so severely with anorexia. My mind was so clouded.

As you know by now, not until I became a mom did I recognize my purpose and have my Wide Awakening. I found that I better shape up to show them that life is a treasure. In college, I developed anorexia to distract myself from finding my life's purpose and then the anorexia became my purpose. How's that for nothing? But really, I now believe it was how my life was supposed to play out . . . that I had to go through something so painful, so sad, and so terrible to come out as strong as I feel right now—and to find my purpose. Helping others by telling my story and teaching yoga and everything I have learned up to this point.

Are you struggling with finding your life's purpose, your calling? What type of person are you? Since we have loosened up some old wounds and eased some pain in the preceding chapters, it may be easier to know what you really want. Keep working on healing your chakras as we did in chapter 8. Your inner strength is evolving. You are coming into who you really are. You are breaking through the chains of anorexia even as you read through this book.

Through my recovery, I have found that our greatest purpose in life is to evolve into a more compassionate, more loving, more giving spiritual being having a human experience. We can do that by having the courage to live our life's purpose, doing things we are good at and things we enjoy to make the world a better, more loving, place to live. Staying at the nine-to-five cubicle job pushing papers around for an overworked, high-powered stress case of a boss most likely is not fulfilling your life's purpose. Or sitting in front of the mirror picking at every flaw is not what our lives were intended to be used for. You are wasting your talent. You have to have faith that God or your Source put you here to fulfill a life purpose. If you are not using your gifts and just dragging your feet through life, you will get the same boring, dragging, struggling day-to-day dullness. The depression pit and the anorexia mind-trap keeps pulling you down.

How to Find Your True Calling

1. Integrate your mind, body, and spirit.

As we discussed in the previous chapters of the book, this integration is where your life lives. Heal the mind by working on your past troubles (which we did in chapters 1-3), honor your body with whole, rich foods (chapter 4) and exercise (chapter 5) in a way that feels good to you. In chapter 6, we developed our Wide-Awake Team. Finally, in chapter 7, we worked on connecting with our spirit. In chapter 8 we combined the mind, body, and spirit through chakra energy healing. Keep rereading until it sticks for you. Don't give up. It's gonna be difficult. You have got to stay strong. Hard work is always rewarded. Always!

2. Find a job you love.

Don't just work for the paycheck! You are working a large percentage of your life. Do work that fuels your passion or at least interests you in some way. I want you to access your wildest dream. I'm not talking about the Porsche or the mansion in Santa Barbara. I'm talking about what you imagine yourself doing where you feel totally and completely head-over-heels in love. Where you lose all track of time, where you feel centered, grateful, and joyful. I am sure you are providing someone with a product you make or a service you offer. Do you make jewelry? Do you talk your friends through hard times? Do you bake cookies for your neighbors, family members, and friends? Take this radical leap of faith! Stop running from your life, and start living it! I am freakin' serious. I can hear the "I can't" voice right now. "I can't leave my job." "What will I do for money?" Whatever you love doing and spend most of your time dreaming about—or even better, doing—make it your job. This is your true calling! This is why you are here on this Earth. No one can do exactly what you do and offer what you offer! If you are fully present and passionate and in love with what you love to do, money will come. If money is not that important to you, another perk to this is that you are happy. Your enthusiasm and love of your chosen job will be infectious. People will pay for your products. They will be swarming to help them live fuller, richer lives through your services. You can do it! You have already forgiven the past with chapters 1-3 and practiced self-love, surrounded yourself with the right people with what we learned in chapter 7, and are working on healing blocked chakras in chapter 8. This is just the final step. I can't promise that it will be easy. But this I know for sure: hard work and passionate work are always rewarded! This is your one and only chance at life. As Dr. Dyer states, "Don't let that music die still inside you." Let it out!

3. Go for it!

I know some of you are going to say no to point 2. "What does she know? I like fishing, and I want to fish all day. You can't make any money doing that!" I say, "Excuse!" There are plenty of fishermen who make a great living and love what they do. Or maybe you could work in a maritime museum educating others on marine life. They are plenty of possibilities. I have seen death too soon and too fast with some of my family members and friends. There are no guarantees in this life. So get busy being happy before it's too late. I am hesitant to use the word "can't," but if you cannot leave your unhappy job for a myriad of reasons, point four may give you an alternate solution.

4. List your greatest joys outside your job.

Do you love playing with kids? Do you like reading romantic novels, watching sports, or playing a musical instrument? Get out your journal and list the top ten things you are joyful about in your life. No fewer than ten! Do those things when you get in from work. Have your loved ones help out with the chores, cooking meals, and cleaning up after themselves. Call a babysitter, neighbor, friend, relative to help out with the kids, if you have any. You are valuable too, and you simply cannot do it all. If everyone chips in, that will free up more time for you to do the things you enjoy. So get out that journal and list your ten most joyful activities, and do at least two of them a day.

At the end of your life, will you be proud of how you lived? Did you give your life your best shot? Don't be afraid to express what you want in life. Rather than being scared of dying, be scared of not living the life you want and deserve! Every day is a gift, and every day we learn. Did you follow your heart and intuition? Make a positive difference in the world with even the smallest acts. Even through your recovery, you can give back by helping others struggling with the disease. When you give of yourself, nothing is ever too small to offer to the world. Something as simple as a smile is a great place to start.

Your journey is not over. You are alive! You still have things to achieve, people to meet, lessons to learn, and opportunities to love.

Epilogue

Whew! You made it!

You may have learned some new things and/or reinforced some ideas you had already been exploring. Learning new things can be scary. You will get there. I promise. What's scarier is repeating the old patterns. Living a life with an eating disorder is not what you are here to do! Growth can only occur when you are open to trying something different! Incorporate these ideas into your life and watch things expand and grow into a gift of sustainable happiness and final recovery from your eating disorder.

This book is all about looking inward. Looking inward can be hard and very painful at times. That's why so many people avoid doing the work—because it's difficult, and it hurts. You are different. You possess the willingness to change. Be proud of that! You are trying, and that is all any of us can do. Your willingness is half the battle. If you keep your mind open each day to expect positive things to come into your life, they will. Stay willing. Stay focused, even during the more challenging moments. Lean on one of your Zen friends or forgiving family members. Keep working hard. Never give up.

Every day, make a moment-by-moment decision to choose to love yourself. If you want to change, you have to accept yourself as you are right now.

You are a success story. You aren't scared to examine yourself and be responsible for your own happiness. You are committed to doing the dirty work for yourself or someone you love by buying this book. You know that you wanted to be healed and to stop engaging in unhealthy habits. You know now that you are on this Earth to grow, learn, change, fail, succeed, and add value to the world. Life is a series of lessons. There is always room for personal growth in all of our journeys.

You now know you don't need to be "fixed." You were born beautiful just the way you are.

You also know that self-love and self-acceptance are the keys to living a full, rich life. Without these, it is difficult to have successful relationships, careers, and good health. Their absence is blocking the shine of your everlasting, beautiful soul.

You have dug deep and are healing old emotional baggage.

You know now that the images in the media aren't real. Corporate giants are selling you this image to make you believe you aren't enough, so you buy their product. You know your outer beauty is only a reflection of the inner beauty you possess.

If you knew how many people you have touched by your presence, you would be shocked. You are so amazing just by being you.

My hope for you is to see yourself as the radiant being you are. Celebrate your uniqueness unapologetically. Love yourself without abandon. Feed yourself whole, nutritious foods. Move your body. Reach Your Wide Awakening, where you let it all finally go.

You have finally gotten up the courage to live the life you deserve. Focus on the progress you have already made. You are doing fantastically. Just relax, breathe, and love yourself today. Focus on where you are headed. Through Your Wide Awakening you will realize you had the strength all along. Just keep being your awesome self.

Success is not measured by what you have accomplished, but by the opposition you have encountered, and the courage with which you have maintained the struggle against overwhelming odds.

—Orson Swett Marden

CPSIA information can be obtained
at www.ICGtesting.com
Printed in the USA
LVHW041322200222
711565LV00004B/163